PIONEERS IN ISRAEL

PIONEERS IN ISRAEL

by
SHMUEL DAYAN

INTRODUCED, EDITED, AND ARRANGED BY
YAËL DAYAN

TRANSLATED FROM THE HEBREW
BY SIDNEY LIGHTMAN

THE WORLD PUBLISHING COMPANY

CLEVELAND AND NEW YORK

Published by The World Publishing Company

2231 West 110th Street, Cleveland 2, Ohio

Library of Congress Catalog Card Number: 61–5806

FIRST EDITION

CONTENTS

v

ILLUSTRATIONS

INTRODUCTION

THIS BOOK is the story of a man, not of a period, but the man represents a period. It is less a historical document than history seen through the eyes and heart of a person who made and lived it.

Shmuel Dayan—a teenage Palestine immigrant in 1908, a pioneer and farmer, and from 1950 a member of the Israel Parliament—wrote five books and many articles and essays in Hebrew.

The material gathered in his writings and letters covers fifty years—from the important emigration from Russia, through the establishment of the Kibbutz (the communal settlement), the establishment of the Moshav (the co-operative settlement), the fight against the Arabs and the British—to the new responsibilities the state of Israel introduced: the assimilation of new immigrants and the creation of one people adjusted to its new land.

I had to choose and select from the written material the chapters and paragraphs which are autobiographical and arrange them chronologically. I have tried to give material on two levels—the personal life story and the ideals behind the way of life this group of people chose; and to fuse the conflicts and clashes between these two—the individual and the group, the private will and the common good.

When we read Utopian writings, from Aristotle to More or Fourier, we realize the gap between the ideal and reality, and accept the plan, philosophy or programme as a social study, not as a way of life. It will not be wrong to say that Shmuel Dayan and the group of people with whom he lived and created, lived their Utopia, carrying out a social plan, living according to a pattern which demanded compromise, which was experimental and succeeded in becoming a practical, feasible way of life for thousands.

Much has been written about Palestine and later Israel. This book if not a substitute for others is an important addition, as it gives the picture seen from inside.

What *did* the individual feel? How did the Russian boy or girl become a 'new type of Jew', why did he compromise? How was it possible to give up privacy and individual outlooks and live in a commune? All these questions are answered here.

My generation, this of the grandchildren, sees in my grandfather's a symbol and an example. We never met the difficulties and challenge they did, and we know that whatever we have in the form of home, state and meaningful life we owe to them, and we do not take it for granted. That is why it was a duty as well as a pleasure to edit and arrange this volume.

YAËL DAYAN

CHAPTER ONE

FROM SOUTH RUSSIA TO THE
LAKE OF TIBERIAS

THERE WERE several hundred Jewish families in Djeskov, in the Kiev region of the Ukraine in Russia. The houses were built of some kind of clay with wooden beams, and many of them were plastered and whitewashed. Their roofs were thatched with straw, renewed in places where it had grown brittle, giving them a striped appearance. The rows of houses were laid out in a rough sort of rectangle and in the open spaces between shops stalls had been erected. Thursday was market day, when the peasants came in from the surrounding countryside in their carts, laden with farm produce and handmade articles. The square was crowded with their horses, their foals, their pigs and their poultry. The air was full of strident noise, and the reek of pitch, resin and alcohol pervaded everything.

The Jews sold the peasants whatever they needed—fish, shoes, ribbons, coloured paper to decorate their houses, tools, farm implements, and clothes. In the evening, the peasants clambered unsteadily onto their carts, drunk, and made their way back to their villages. The Jews closed their shops, and the empty square resumed its usual state, looking like a deserted battlefield. The end of market day was also the end of any contact between the Jews and their non-Jewish neighbours except for the rare occasions when a horse-drawn carriage drove up to one of the bigger shops, bringing the wife of one of the local gentry. She would step down from her carriage and be received with a great deal of bowing by the shopkeeper and his assistants, who hurried to supply her wants.

In the main part of the town, behind the Jewish houses, the non-Jews lived in small, low houses set in gardens full of flowers and trees. Chickens scratched about and cackled, and cattle wandered about the fenced yards. The Jewish and non-Jewish areas were quite separate, although some brave Jews did mix with the non-Jews, transacting all kinds of shady business with them. These Jews were feared by other Jews, non-Jews and officials alike. There were some brothers, living with their mother, who were mixed up in all kinds of roguery. To their credit be it said, however, that whenever there was any sort of quarrel between Jews and non-Jews, they always came to the aid of their brethren. Jewish artisans lived in the lanes and side turnings, and they were a group on their own.

The old synagogue, a squat building, was in the main street, while the new prayer-hall was in a side lane. This was the head-quarters of the progressive elements of the town, where the young men dressed in ordinary clothes and without side-curls. Here they used to gather and say their prayers quickly. Not for them the long drawn-out services of the synagogue, the glass of wine to celebrate a birth or a Bar-Mitzvah. The young lads came early and helped the Rabbi's wife to put the room in order before the service started. The young girls stayed at home scouring the pots and pans and polishing the candlesticks, while their mothers hurried to the market, handkerchiefs round their heads, and baskets in their hands. When the Sabbath came, quietness reigned and the only non-Jew to be seen in the Jewish quarter was the Sabbath-goy who turned out the lamps for a slice of chala (Sabbath bread) and a glass of Sabbath wine, raising his hat and accepting them grate-fully. The table was covered with a clean white cloth, the chala laid out ready under a small coloured napkin. The men put on their long, black, shiny coats and wore a black sash tied round their waists. They would set out for the synagogue with slow, measured steps, their sons who were not yet Bar-Mitzvah carrying their prayer books and prayer shawls.

The cantor started the service, chanting with his prayer shawl draped over his head, and the congregation sang the responses.

At the reading of the Law, a preacher would mount the rostrum and give a sermon. After prayers were over, everyone would leave the synagogue, busily discussing politics and Zionism. Everyone would go to one of the houses to drink a glass of wine to celebrate a wedding or some other joyful occasion, and then all of us would make our way home for Sabbath lunch, followed by a good sleep in the afternoon. While their parents slept, the children played. Some people went for a walk as far as the new railway which had been built near the sugar factory. Young men and girls also went walking there. There it was also that one heard Russian spoken by the intelligentsia— the doctor, the chemist, and the other professional men.

As the Sabbath began to draw to a close, sadness would steal into people's hearts and deep sighs would escape them. Another week was beginning, another week of hard work and worry about earning a living.

The bitterness of exile in the Diaspora showed itself in their eyes, and the same old question possessed their minds—'Where shall I find rest?'

All our family lived together. Grandfather, Rabbi Pinhas Dayan, was tall and erect, with a slow stately gait. He spent all his time poring over the Bible and other learned Jewish books, and reading the various commentaries on them. At intervals, he would walk up and down the hall in his white felt slippers with his dressing gown swirling about him. On his head he wore a broad-brimmed hat over the silk skull cap which he never took off, even at night. Round his neck was the small prayer shawl every religious Jew wears—the fringed garment or Tsitsit, that the children of Israel were commanded to wear in the Book of Numbers (xv 37–39)—and it came down to his knees. The Gemara was always open in front of him, even when he was resting from his studies for a while.

Leading off the hall where Grandfather lived, there were the rooms where his four sons lived with their families. On market day the hall would be filled with visitors—relatives, friends, acquaintances, people with messages, marriage brokers, and ordinary poor people. They had all come to have their usual market day lunch. Grandfather sat at the head of the table and poured a glass of wine for everyone, while Grandmother Rachel served plates of hot beetroot soup with meat cut up in it, followed by roast meat

3

with a thick floury sauce. Everyone set to with appetite, and conversation flowed freely round the table.

Although the community had an official Rabbi who was its spiritual head, not everyone went to him for advice. Many came to my grandfather to consult him on business and personal matters, as well as religious questions, and he never betrayed a confidence. Whenever a visiting rabbi came to the town he stayed in Grandfather's house. Everyone would come to shake the rabbi's hand or just touch his fingertips, and would go away feeling comforted and with hope of better days ahead.

My father, Avraham Dayan, was an unlucky man. When he was a child he had somehow got into the middle of a herd of cows and a bull had attacked him, breaking his leg, so that he always walked with a limp. He did not want to become a ritual slaughterer like his father, Pinhas, and deliberately threw the special slaughtering knife on the ground to break the blade and spoil it so that it could not be used. Instead he decided to become a business man. He went into partnership with someone, got deeply into debt, and had to wind up the partnership. He was left without a farthing and without any means of earning a living in Djeskov, so he and his family of eight went to Odessa.

He was an honest man and a lover of truth, was not obsequious, and fought against injustice. All he wanted to do was to set up as a shopkeeper so that he could be independent of other people's assistance, but he was dogged by misfortune and could not make a success of anything.

The family were grief-stricken when the two-year-old, the child of our parents' old age, died. I was only five then, and they sent me back to Grandfather's house. Eventually they all came back, and Father became a commercial traveller.

As for me, my heart was not in studying the Torah, the Holy Law. They sent me to cheder (Hebrew religious classes) but I did not learn very much, and at the age of thirteen became an assistant to my father, who used to travel round to the various merchants, selling them cloth. Father trusted me, and I also had an aptitude for business, so every Monday I used to go to the main city of the region, Oman, to buy the cloth our clients had ordered, returning a day or two later. I used to ride on one of the wagons laden with boxes, bales, sacks and barrels, which constituted our road haulage service. We would deliver the cloth on Thursday and send in our bills on Fridays. On Sundays we collected new orders. On Mondays, I would go off to Oman again, and so on.

I became a real commercial traveller, and Ivan the carter used to prepare a special place for me on his wagon on some soft straw. His horses were well fed and beautifully looked after, but he was always rather drunk.

My parents made me wear a black fur coat with an enormous collar, and a wide red sash round my middle. I was so muffled up inside the coat that no part of me was visible at all, and it was so big and heavy that I had to have help to take it off. In the pocket I kept our orders and the money for the cloth I had to buy to fill them.

I worked six days a week, but on Saturdays I needed some sort of spiritual sustenance. At home, even then, copies of *Hatzefira* and Zionist pamphlets could be found interspersed with the holy books which constituted our library. A Zionist preacher gave a sermon in the synagogue. A Bund meeting was held in secret in the loft. After the Kishinev pogroms we studied Bialik's poems. The death of Herzl was a sad blow.

I was 16 years old, and began to wonder where my life was leading. I was surrounded by an atmosphere of depression and uncertainty. Everyone was talking about the non-Jews' hatred of us in the Duma. Then a few copies of *Hapoel Hatzair* came into my hands. Yosef Vitkin's articles opened my eyes. 'Our people is sick. Come to Palestine, where you are needed!' And there was a short article by Hararit, its theme going straight to my heart: 'Mule drivers, shepherds, you will be like Rabbi Akiva was!' Then and there I decided that I would help to build my country, my motherland. But how could I do it, and how could I get there? 'The land of the Jordan and Mount Hermon, of Jerusalem and the Cave of Machpela, and the Dead Sea'. I dreamed of all these places, but when I mentioned my ambition to the family they regarded it as a joke. Just the same, my resolve grew stronger, and the journey began.

In June 1908 I arrived off Jaffa in a Russian cargo ship, and my journey at an end, I transferred to a small boat. Before I had had time to collect my thoughts, the boat had completed its rocky passage, and I was put ashore in Jaffa. The sandy wastes all around, and the Arabs with their strange dress and guttural cries all added to my bewilderment. As I stood there my heart was filled with doubt and disappointment.

When my passport was taken from me and I was given a red form in exchange I realised that I had now come under the sway of a new authority—that of the fez and the strange writing on the form. It was an unhappy moment for me and for my companions, but our hearts were lightened by two fellow-Jews who had come down to the shore to receive us. One was a representative of the Jaffa branch of the Odessa Committee and the other a hotel owner.

We followed them, a porter preceding us with our luggage slung across his shoulders. As we negotiated the dark twisting lanes of the town, camels passed us with their bells jingling. All around us donkeys were braying, and the air was full of smells. Veiled Arab women passed by, and over all could be heard the strident voices and rattling copper mugs of the cold drink sellers.

The scene changed suddenly as we came to a courtyard and passed through it into a large hall with rooms leading off on two sides. Tables and benches had been put up and ran the length of the hall with its latticed windows. All round us stood bearded men and youths, the hotel owner and his wife in their midst, asking us all kinds of questions and telling us what had been happening in Jaffa.

There had been riots there, they said, and showed us broken windows to prove it.

We set off for the Odessa Committee's office to see if there was any work. I had taken off my coat and was dressed Russian style in a black shirt buttoned up to the neck, and with a cord tied round my middle to serve as a belt. 'Russian', the Arabs called after me, as I made my way to the office. 'There is work at Petach Tikva', we were told.

My sister, meanwhile had been given a letter recommending her as an assistant to a tailor in Jerusalem, so we took her to the railway station and set off to find the diligence (stage-coach) to Petach Tikva. Our fellow passengers were well-dressed farmers, loaded with shopping they were bringing back from town. They spoke a different Yiddish from us.

The journey took three hours, and as there was no made-up road, the diligence often got stuck in the sand. We passed many black Beduin tents on the way, their owners standing beside them holding rifles and revolvers. The countryside was open, empty and wide, with the hills and villages of Judaea in the distance. Adjoining the settlement were citrus groves, vineyards, and almond plantations, surrounded by rows of cactus plants (the well-known prickly pear or sabra). Arabs, men and women, were walking about the paths in the groves, and from time to time a Jew would ride among them on a horse or donkey.

Then we saw the white houses of Petach Tikva.

The diligence stopped in the centre of the settlement and was immediately surrounded by a crowd of people wanting news and letters. Our baggage was put off at Shabetai Rabinowitz's workers' hostel, and we stood looking about us at the lively scene. Young men were dancing in the street and one of the new immigrants immediately took a violin out of his luggage, and began to accompany them. Soon we were drawn into the circle of dancers and that was our introduction and our induction to the workers of Petach Tikva.

In the centre of the room at the workers' hostel stood a table surrounded by planks supported on paraffin cans. They served as benches by day and beds by night.

Every time we had a meal, we were also eating up our money. All I had was half a gold Napoleon, having given the other half to my sister, the one who had gone to Jerusalem. I had been given a Napoleon (twenty gold French francs) for the ten Russian roubles which were all I had left by the time I had been through the customs in Jaffa. Before my half-Napoleon had entirely vanished, however, we had a stroke of luck. A Jew came into the hostel asking for workers for the next day, and we volunteered. I spent an uncomfortable night on my bed of boards, waiting for dawn and my first day of work in Palestine. The settlement's great bell tolled, and I got up. I filled my haversack with a round loaf still warm from the bakery, dates, a bit of greenstuff wrapped in paper, a few olives, and some salt. Then I set out for the field where I was to work that day.

When I got there, I found scores of Arabs at work harvesting corn, while a Jew walked up and down among them urging them on with cries of 'Yalla, yalla!' I was given a rake and put to work in an adjoining barley-field where the barley had already been cut.

B

7

After showing me how to do the work, the owner of the field went off and I was left on my own. My fingers began to swell, my head ached and my body trembled with fever. The sun beat down on me and flies swarmed all round. Their buzzing and stinging drove me almost to the point of madness. Meanwhile, the Arabs sang as they worked, and I who had come with the aim of winning work from them, sank steadily lower in my own esteem.

I exhorted myself to continue, for I had to work and learn from experience. In the shade of some tall, spreading eucalyptus trees, stood some paraffin tins filled with water. Eucalyptus leaves had been dropped into the water as a specific against malaria. The Arabs drank this liquid, and I followed their example. The smell of the paraffin made me feel sick and the taste of the eucalyptus leaves was like wormwood in my mouth, but I clenched my hands on my rake and kept on working. I took off my shirt and wrapped it round my head and ears to keep the flies off, but they continued buzzed round me, looking for uncovered strips of flesh. Finally, the bell rang for the midday break, redeeming me from my labours. The Jew called to me to come and sit next to him while we ate, and gave me a tomato, the first one I had ever seen in my life. At the first taste I felt sick and lay prostrate and fainting under the eucalyptus trees, while the Arabs sat around and jeered at me.

In the evening I received my first day's wages, seven piastres, in the form of a small piece of pasteboard on which was printed, 'Token, 7 piastres, Petach Tikva Settlement Council'. This token gave me fresh courage because it proved that I had earned my bread by the sweat of my brow.

I lay down to sleep on my planks, racked with hot and cold shivers. My teeth chattered and my tongue was dry. In the morning I tried to stand up and fell flat on my face. My companions immediately dosed me with quinine, laughing and commiserating with me, while I lay there with a mist before my eyes. I fell into a fitful sleep, waking up and dropping off again at intervals. I had malaria. 'Never mind,' they said, 'malaria is not a serious illness'.

My sister Beilah returned from Jerusalem, because the tailor had no work for her. We packed our bags and moved to a room in a narrow side turning. Our plan was for her to be a housewife while we all went out to work. We all had malaria, but there was nothing to be done about it. It was Shevuot (Pentecost) and we could hear singing and dancing going on outside. I lay there in a fever, sweating and weak, and seemed to see a vision of my mother and father, weeping bitterly for us. I felt sorry for them and for myself and tears began to fall from my eyes also.

We got better, and again went out to look for work. In the centre of the township near the synagogue we stood early one morning. Employers came, engaged Arab workers and left us standing there. There was nothing for it but to return to our empty room, shamefaced and with nothing to eat.

That evening when the diligence arrived from Jaffa, it brought us our first letters from home. We read and re-read them with excitement; how our parents were missing us, lots of kisses from both, and please to come home. But we had burnt our bridges.

In the morning we went out looking for work again. The market was nearby, filled with hundreds of buyers and sellers—the buyers Jewish, the sellers Arab. Vegetables, chickens, greenstuff, grain, fodder, straw, charcoal, wood—it was all there waiting to be sold and bought. Jewish money was flowing into the Arab villages, for they were the suppliers of food and other commodities. The men of the villages were the workers and the labourers and they were also the educators of the farmers' children. From their childhood the sons of the Biluim learnt Arab songs and Arab ways and the Arab tongue.

Meanwhile I was working in an orchard, digging shallow holes for irrigation or deepening existing ones. They were a strange shape, neither round nor square, and I did not stick to any particular row of trees but wandered from one to another without any method. The more experienced workers discussed this among themselves and evolved a plan. They tied some string to my body and secured the other end to the last tree in the row, so that I no longer wandered about haphazardly but worked in a straight line. My hands became cracked and inflamed and touching a spade was agony, but the older workers urged me to persevere. They said that my hands would harden and the pain would disappear. I worked on.

We sprayed the trees with an acrid liquid against black beetle. The strong workers held the rubber hose, and I had to pull the hand-cart, whose two wheels sank deep into the sand at every step. I was young and a tyro, but I gritted my teeth and pulled that hand-cart. Droplets of acrid spray fell on me continuously, my skin began to peel and flake, and my clothes reeked of the strong liquid; but I pressed on till the job was finished, even though I was still in the grip of malaria.

I decided to change both place and work and went to Rehovot to do guard duty in the vineyards. This was to be my convalescence—a change of air, a rest, and plenty of grapes to eat. Rehovot was a busy settlement, and had some forty watchmen guarding the vineyards. The strong, experienced ones guarded the perimeter while the not-so-strong beginners patrolled inside. The watchmen on duty outside the vineyards had rifles and revolvers, while all I had was a stout cane with a knob at the end. A hole had been bored in it, through which was threaded a knotted thong, so that the cane could be swung from the wrist like a truncheon.

The owner of the particular vineyard where I was on duty supplied us with planks and beams and we put up watchmen's huts ten feet high or so. The planks served as a kind of platform from which the surrounding area could be observed. During the night the watchmen patrolled among the vines, and when dawn came, they stretched out on mats in the hut and slept. I made my first round of the vineyard with great conscientiousness, marking out the limits of my patrol. When sleep threatened, I would approach the neighbouring guard and converse with him in whispers. We whistled shrilly to frighten off jackals, and shouted to try out neighbouring watchmen and see if they would come to our assistance. Meanwhile, right in the middle of the vineyards the old hands would engage in nightlong discussions, in which they were always joined by girls from the settlement. We lived on bread and grapes and a little salt fish, and there was cold water in a jug in the hut.

The vineyard watchmen's job finished when the grapes had been harvested and the vines stripped bare. The pickers' baskets lay among the vines and along the paths, and the huts were deserted. We were no longer needed in the settlement. What were we to do? With some of the money I had saved from my wages as a watchman I bought a pair of shoes. The two Napoleons left over, I wrapped in a handkerchief and put in my pocket.

It was at that time, the summer of 1908, that Turkey's constitution was proclaimed, and as devoted citizens we wanted to participate in the celebrations. When we reached Jaffa speeches were being made from a beflagged dais in front of Government House, and there were two Jews among the orators. One of them became so enthusiastic that he took off his shoes and auctioned them for the benefit of the State, to the accompaniment of cheers from the Arab audience.

I was looking for work again, now feeling stronger and more at home, and went to the small settlement of Ein Ganim. In my small room the only piece of furniture was a mat on the floor. I slept on it, ate on it, rested and read on it. I also had a clay oven with its bed of glowing coals, and on it stood an earthenware pot filled with chick peas, salt and water. The pot would be put on at midnight, and by morning the chick peas would be soft, making a very satisfying food. After work, when I was tired and hungry, I used to boil some noodles which did not take long to cook, and eat bread and coconut oil with them. For dessert there were prickly pears in the summer and oranges in the winter. We used to take the prickly pears and roll them about in the sand, using a long pole with a nail stuck in the end of it, This treatment used to get rid of the prickles. The main difficulty, however, was the bread. A loaf was small and soft and you swallowed it down in a moment, without being really satisfied. When you had an hour's walk to work in the citrus grove, you kept eating slices of bread, and by the time you got there it was all gone.

My room also served as a meeting place for Hapoel Hatzair (The Young Socialist Jewish Workers' Movement) on Saturdays, as well as being a hostel for workers passing through, who used to come there to sleep. There was no lock on the door. What would have been the point?

In Petach Tikva there was a workers' club which was the meeting place of all the immigrant workers. Lectures were given there by Jewish writers, and it also served as a sort of labour exchange. The habitués of the club used to pass on to each other any details of work available. You could have a glass of tea and a cake at a reasonable price and sit and talk with friends there. Sometimes a girl from the settlement, greatly daring, would come to a lecture, one of the young men would take her fancy, and they would start going about together. So the club was a meeting place for people from two different worlds—girls from the settlement and new immigrants burning with idealism and longing to find work, but unemployed and needing someone to give them inspiration and warmth. It was cosy in the club, and pleasant, in spite of being noisy and crowded.

In the library of the settlement council building one could sit until midnight, summer and winter, and the librarian would offer all that he had at his disposal. I read and read though I did not always understand everything, for some of the expressions in the language were strange to me. But it was good to be the last to leave, together with the librarian himself, because the thirst for knowledge was stronger even than my tiredness after a day's work, and as I was unused to physical work, reading balanced it somehow.

Ein Ganim was the first independent workers' settlement. The settlers built it up by spare-time work before they left for their jobs in Petach Tikva in the morning and after their jobs ended in the evening. They were proud of what they had built up by their own efforts, and they were among the best of all the Jewish workers in Palestine. Many well-known names are to be found among the list of settlers at Ein Ganim—A. D. Gordon, the philosopher Berl Katzenelson, David Shimoni, the poet Y. H. Brenner.

Our central aim was to achieve the rate of work of the Arabs and attain the same rate of pay. If we could compete successfully with them we could help to increase the number of Jewish employed. And these, when experienced and proved, set up our independent settlements. This we could do only after we had proved we could compete with Arab labour, after we had acquired land, and gathered the right group of people to settle independently. So we worked away at pulling up couch-grass from the sandy soil of the citrus groves, doing the same as the scores of Arab labourers.

They turned over the soil with their mattocks, and whenever they saw couch-grass, they immediately pulled it up and put it in a basket. Not a scrap could be missed, because even the tiniest piece left in the ground would grow again and spread. The skilled Arabs tried in various ways to discourage us, but we would not be deterred and did whatever they did. If they sang in rhythm with their work, 'Ya hai lili, ya hai lili', we sang with them, obstinately and with fervour. In shirt and trousers, and with a kefiyeh on my head, I worked and sang. The Arabs began to tire, and since they recognised our determination not to be beaten, they stopped trying to

beat us. The grove owner and his Jewish foreman also acknow-
ledged our endurance.

Malaria still raged in my body and would not leave me. Every
afternoon my temperature rose to 104, but at midnight it dropped
sharply, and I would start shivering and feel waves of weakness
sweeping over me. I would get up, refresh myself and lie down
again until it was morning, and time to go to work in the grove.
If I had a bout of fever during work I used to go and lie down in
the empty packing house where boxes, baskets and tarpaulins
were scattered about. An old Arab woman used to come to my aid.
She was the wife of the watchman, who lived all year round in the
grove with his family. She used to cover me with a tarpaulin and
bring me a cup of hot sweet tea.

For three years I used to get attacks at regular intervals and
quinine became part of my daily diet. The doctor told me, 'There
is only one way out. You must leave the country, because otherwise you will never overcome it.' This was the one piece of advice
none of us could afford to take.

I stayed on at Petach Tikva. I loved the citrus groves whose soil
I watered with my sweat. I planted saplings and saw them grow to
maturity. I felt that I had played a part in their growth and was
happy. I loved the almond plantations too, where I worked sometimes, uprooting couch-grass and harvesting the nuts; and the
sandy paths of the vineyards. I loved the granary where we spent
our evenings and Saturdays, talking or holding debates. I loved,
too, the path from Ein Ganim to Petach Tikva along which I used
to walk every evening, returning at midnight after solid hours of
reading in the library.

Two years passed in this way, and I became an expert with a tur-
iya (long handled spade). A skilled worker now, I travelled about
between Petach Tikva, Ein Ganim and Kfar Saba. I kept my
friendship going, however, with the workers of Ein Ganim.

To work, and work hard, became a matter of great national
economic importance for us. It was a way of expressing our Zionism, more than the writing of essays or making speeches, at a time
when the employers did not believe in our ability and could not pay
us higher wages than they paid Arab labour. There was only one
way out—to become contractors.

The manager of a fifty-dunam citrus grove in Hadera gave us

the contract for cultivating the grove, carrying out guard duties and doing other sundry jobs. Our group included two women as well as some men, among whom were myself and Yosef Weitz.

Our first year was eminently satisfactory and our joy knew no bounds. We established contact with the workers as well as with the farmers of Hadera, in whom a spark of idealism still burnt. This was also the first year of Hashomer, which aimed at training Jews to be watchmen and was a semi-military organization, and the second year of the Hadera commune. The girls of the settlement used to ride its boundaries at night with the watchmen. The workers used to hold meetings and debates. Ahad Ha'am was invited to one of them, but his vision of a spiritual centre for all Jewry did not suffice for us, and the long discussions on this and other subjects became the very stuff of our lives.

One evening Israel Shohat, the head of Hashomer, came to the workers' club and asked for candidates for a Workers' Federation, which would be an auxiliary organisation of Hashomer. I felt that my help might be needed and put my name down; I did not have long to wait. The warning bell pealed out, and we learned that Hashomer had found Arab flocks in our fields and that their Arab shepherds were resisting efforts to drive them out. One of the watchmen rode out after them and we rushed to help. We routed the shepherds, and rounded up the sheep, bringing them back to the settlement in triumph as spoils of war.

Petach Tikva was still our centre, and the journey there on foot from Hadera and back became a matter of routine. We used to set out from Petach Tikva barefoot, our shoes tied together and slung from the scarf knotted round our shoulders, and with revolvers stuck in our belts. We passed through the Arab villages of Kalkilya and Kakun, and six hours later arrived at our destination, footsore and tired. How we appreciated our Sabbath rest. We still had work to do in Kfar Saba, in the young almond plantation, so we slept in the one and only large wooden cabin.

On Saturday night we used to set out in a group for Kfar Saba, haversacks slung over our shoulders, and packed with coconut oil, bread, sugar, apples, a blanket and an old jacket. We would stride on in silence through mud and puddles, the sweat pouring down our faces. Two and a half hours later we would reach the big cabin, stretch out on the floor and sleep soundly.

We were awakened by the boss who put a burning cigarette paper to our toes. At a table in the corner the owner of our lodgings was already pouring out glasses of tea, which cost less without sugar. We ate our meal standing up, mattocks slung across our shoulders, ready to go and dig holes for planting almond trees and to grub up couch-grass growing where saplings had not taken.

The yellow reeds and yellow sand all round us did not offer much inspiration or encouragement. Nevertheless, our six-day working week passed quickly and on Friday afternoon we left Kfar Saba behind us once again, striding out towards Petach Tikva and Hadera with our empty knapsacks on our shoulders, singing and happy.

But our revolvers were a symbol of the times we lived in. While our work in Petach Tikva was in full swing we heard rumours that the Beduin of Zevah had attacked the nearby Jewish settlement of Miskha and that help was needed there. Some thirty of our comrades went up to Galilee. But how could I go up to Galilee when I was completely unarmed?

In the Jaffa market I saw Arabs selling weapons. When someone wanted to try out a revolver he was thinking of buying, he fired at paraffin cans filled with sand. I bought a five-chambered revolver and a full cartridge belt. They were heavy, but I was proud of them. From then onwards I wore my revolver all day at work and at night it was always within easy reach under my pillow. If Kalkilya attacked Kfar Saba, we ran to help, and because of my revolver I was always one of the first to intervene in any set-to between Jews and Arabs. Then, one day, I went up to Galilee, an area inhabited by Arabs. It would have been easier to remain near Jaffa, but we meant to expand and settle and work in the more remote part of the country.

Yavniel lay to the west, its two rows of houses straddling a sloping hillside. The street was narrow and paved with black rock which was difficult to walk on There were low stone walls in front of the houses and by each one a scanty little garden, cows and oxen, calves and heifers, hens and ducks—and pigeons in the dovecote. Here and there lived an Arab and his family.

In the morning twilight, the gates were opened and the goats skipped into the open, the ducks quacked, the calves lowed, the sheep bleated and the mules, harnessed to their carts, clip-clopped their way along the stony road. The heifers were driven out to the fields, and everyone else followed them, ready for the day's work, with ploughs and other implements clinking as they walked.

Everyone scattered to different fields. I sat on a cart, the reins in my hand. In my cart there was fodder for the cattle, and majdera (a sort of porridge made from wheat and lentils) in a pot covered with a towel for me. In a basket I had some pittot (flat Arab loaves), olives and dates. In covered barrels there was water for men and cattle. My workmate, old Ahmed, came with me to the fields to teach me ploughing. The mules also helped me, because the right-hand one, the leader, did not need any tugs on the reins to keep moving along the furrows. And so I became a ploughman.

One bright winter's day I was out ploughing, my right hand on the plough handle, my whip held high, and the mules plodding forward. The black earth was turning under the plough, covering as it turned, the wheat being sown by Ahmed. I burst into song. Here I was ploughing the soil of the land of Israel, what more could my soul want!

As dusk fell we returned to the farmyard, tired and weary, passed through the gate, and unharnessed the mules. We watered them at a stone trough and tethered them to the stalls. Then we sieved their fodder to remove the coarse straw, sand and dust from it. They swallowed their fodder eagerly and we watched them with pleasure because we had become attached to them. Then I turned and went to have my evening meal with the farmer, who asked me all about the day's ploughing and sowing. I slept in the stables as a precaution against thieves, and also so that I could get up and feed the heifers twice a night. Twice the animals got entangled in their chains and would have strangled themselves if I had not gone to their aid. Although I slept, my ears were attuned to every sound.

I was proud of my promotion in rank. Here I was, a worker in Galilee, a kefiyeh round my head, brown boots on my feet, a revolver in my belt and a whip in my hand, driving mules.

From Yavniel to the Sea of Galilee is an uphill climb over rough ground, through wild plum trees and thorn bushes which tear at the eyes. I held tight to my gun in case there was someone lurking in the shadows. I reached the summit of the mountain, and there was the Sea of Galilee spread before me like a burnished mirror, smooth and soft as silk, a pleasure to look upon. The sun was reflected in its sparkling waters and I stood wonder-struck at the sight of it.

The surrounding mountains are a sullen black. Black basalt rocks are scattered about as if they have at this moment been spewed up from the centre of the earth by some erupting volcano. To the eastwards, the mountains are steep and crumpled-seeming, for the floods have scored deep gashes in their sides. They tower over Galilee like sentinels. From there I could also see the Jordan as it flows out of Kinneret—the Sea of Galilee.

After working at Yavniel for six months, and when the sowing was over in the spring, I got a job on an estate. We transported olive trees from the nursery in carts, and planted them on some scores of dunams of land on the mountain-side. We called it Kerem Dessau, because the Jews of Dessau in Germany had contributed towards it. I lodged in the motor-room about a mile and a quarter from the farm, together with Eliezer Jaffé of the Young Farmer organisation. Every morning we used to take the boxes we slept on and throw them outside, and then wrestle with all our might with the huge flywheel of the motor, turning it slowly, while the motor steadfastly refused to fire.

On the estate itself, we were a lively crowd. Laughter and jokes resounded, often at the foreman's expense. The girls of Hannah Maisel's school had white kefiyehs. They loved laughter and dancing, and sometimes there was music on Saturday night.

On Saturdays there was a special routine. The fortunate one among us would saddle Rachvan the little white horse, mount him, and go trotting off to Avadiah, Tiberias or Um-Juni. What greater Sabbath pleasure could there be! Often, very early in the morning, the young men and the girls would go up the mountain, while everything was still wet with dew and mist was thick all around. Afterwards they would hurry back down and have an early morning swim in the lake.

It was then that I met Rachel, who later became one of our national poets. I found her within the boundary wall, the only one in the surrounding wilderness, among a community of a few score souls. She was upright and radiant, tender in years, and her eyes were big and deep. Her clear voice was like a refreshing breeze, and her sparkling laugh made the heart glad. She radiated youthfulness and vigour, and infused everyone with her spirit wherever she went and whatever she did.

She was not born a country girl, but had been brought up and educated in the city, and had come straight from her studies. Her thirst for knowledge had not deserted her even on the estate, and she was always to be found with a book under her arm. She had uprooted all desires and inclinations from her heart and was possessed by only one thing—her unceasing yearning for plants, flowers and birds. She was rooted like a tender plant in the blessed land of Galilee, the land of her birth. In those days we were a band of comrades, and in our devotion to the country we said that anyone who left it was like a man running away in battle. Every single person who left the country, left the mark of his failure on the workers who stayed.

If any of us had not seen each other for some time, we used to write letters to each other—in a short letter to Rachel, I set down my feelings about her going abroad. She replied from Kinneret before leaving for France.

This is what I wrote to her:

'Full of bright anticipation, you are leaving Galilee and going far away from Kinneret and the Jordan. Was it impossible to do anything else? I remain here alone in this wonderful place, but my eyes will seek after you—whether in envy or yearning I do not know. You are leaving Galilee and work—the joys of your youth. You were a worker once but now you are not. And will you still be aware of our world, the world of the workers? Will you remember and understand? Yes, you will have studied for another three years, and as for us . . . Are you going to vanish from before our eyes and not return?'

Rachel replied:

'Why your lamentations for me, my dear? I am not dead yet. Your words saddened me, Shmuel. Your lack of understanding grieved me. Why then do you think I am going abroad? Don't you know that it is in order to become proficient in my work, to become bound up in it with every fibre of heart and brain, to probe the secrets of every growing thing? Is it wrong to breathe the spirit of life into the dusty earth, to beautify and adorn the face of my country? Are these things not to be done? Am I not to leave now and

return at the end of two years? I shall return in the springtime,
full of longing and of yearning for the time that has passed. For I
have taken an oath to my lake, my mountains and my river Jordan!'

Later, she wrote to me from France:

'Shalom to you, Shmuel.

'I want you to know that this postcard is only a forerunner,
heralding a whole host of fat letters. It is essential, however, that
the herald's proclamation should be echoed by an answering
voice. Can you believe that six months have already passed since
we parted on the shore of our Kinneret? But time has wings . . .
it is a year since I travelled the length and breadth of Palestine,
and now here I am in Toulouse, a city with the charm of the
south, but whose skies are not the skies of my country. I have
enrolled at the Agricultural Institute and I shall fall upon my
studies like a ravening wolf. There is another Palestinian studying
here, so we shall be able to ease the bitterness of things for each
other a little. Please write to me, Shmuel, and tell me how you are
and give me all your news. I wish you all the best forever.'

Since I am concerned with Rachel in this chapter, I shall include here a later letter of hers, written in 1921 (when she was in
Safed with T.B.) to my wife Devora:

'A new era has begun here in hospital in Safed. There is a good
side even to this depressing place. There are all kinds of new im-
pressions to enrich the soul. Finally, there comes that blessed
feeling of getting used to things, and then everything begins to
improve. I cannot conceal the fact, however, that my first day here
was hard to bear. I found it particularly difficult to endure wearing
hospital clothes, which make everybody look the same and blur
individual differences. Only then did I realise that I am not a demo-
crat. (I would not reveal this dreadful fact to just anyone, by the
way).

'My day begins at five, as in the Kibbutz. The difference is
that here a day is at least forty-eight hours long. I lie down, get up,
lie down again, chatter, fall silent—and still the heartless clock
shows only ten o'clock. There are people who would commit
murder for the chance of a rest like this, but I am a woman of
temperament and it is disastrous for me.

'What a beautiful spot this is to walk along the paths of the mountainside with a breeze from the summit blowing in your face. Oh

Devora, Devora, what endless vistas life offers. But suddenly, fate says "Only as far as here!" It is a strange thing, but my thoughts no longer have the strength to burst through the barrier. They too have donned hospital garments.

'Stranger still is the fact that despite everything, I have felt my physical self improving . . . The same lively feeling of activity that courses through a healthy person's veins as soon as he gets up in the morning, is beginning to course through my veins as well. But I am deceiving it, by reading. I have all the books I want, thanks to Dr. K. Yes, it is the same Dr. K. who broke the hearts of all the Hadassah nurses, or at least cracked them. Apart from reading, I am busy with plans for the future. Do you know what I am going to do when I get better? I am going to work at Kfar Giladi. Sarah Hankin is in my ward here, and we have arranged it between us. Of course, the winter will drive me out of there southwards, but there will be some pleasant months. Upper Galilee has always epitomised Israel for me, and stirred in me that intense feeling one has for one's homeland. There is a special kind of strength there which opposed tremendous forces in the old days of long ago. Now they are going to give me a sun bath. I told the nurse that I still have a reserve of sun from Degania, but she doesn't want to include that in the reckoning, so we shall have to part, Devora my dear friend.

'Goodbye now, and think of me. My regards to Mussik and Shmuel, and to Degania.

Yours,
Rachel.

P.S.   I have to admit that this letter is not written with my life's blood. In this prosaic era even poets use ink.'

CHAPTER TWO

THE KIBBUTZ

The commune seemed the solution on the eve of the first World War. Lack of security, lack of working facilities, political and social limitations, all could be overcome if a group of people, a small group, would live together, each giving whatever he could and receiving whatever he needed. Work, equality, simplicity, were the corner stones of the system, and Degania was established.

The writer does not describe the ideals, as much as the way of life—later, and to this day, attracting many youngsters and setting an example for new communes. The letters included are of interest not only because of their autobiographical value, but because it is strange to realise how important was the place that communal affairs took in the most intimate letters, in every step the individual made.

Degania is situated on the southern shore of Lake Tiberias, with good soil, River Jordan water and unbearable heat. In 1912 there were two buildings and a small farm. Today it is one of the wealthiest and most advanced settlements in Israel.

In spite of its relative wealth, modern way of life and comfort, it is still a commune, based on the 1912 ideas and ideals, facing socially similar problems and solving them the way they were solved before. In 1912 it was an experiment, in 1960 it is a certainty.

The buildings were finished but we were in no hurry to move in, for it was hard to take leave of our makeshift accommodation at

Um-Juni. The new buildings were a sign that our life would now be more profitable and less toilsome. It was as if idealism and the pioneering spirit had come to an end, to be replaced by the beginning sof a material life. We were in no hurry, and made the transition without much enthusiasm, as if it were just another job to be done.

This was on Friday, 1st May, 1912. Some of the members of the kibbutz, men and women, transferred all our belongings, while the rest worked in the fields. Some of us stayed on guard in the fields all night as well. In the morning, tea or milk would be brought out to the guard, and again in the afternoon. They would stay in the fields, and nobody would return home until evening, except on Saturdays, when work finished in the morning. At about nine o'clock we would go home, not to Um-Juni, but to Degania.

At that time we were still discussing and deciding whether our group was to be a 'settlement kibbutz' or a 'pioneering kibbutz'. These were the early days of the first settlement in the Jezreel Valley, Merhavia. They were days of hope, and the prospect of redeeming the soil. Some of our members felt in their hearts the urge to be pioneers, to conquer new land, redeem fresh soil. They looked with envy at Merhavia, whose members were redeeming the soil of the Emek (Valley, i.e. Jezreel Valley), and dreamed of doing the same themselves, preparing land so that new settlements could be founded on it. Our duty was to conquer. We were fighters, the pioneering vanguard, preparing the soil for the nation that was to come after us. How we yearned for that life, the life of conquerors!

At that time, we were fascinated by Horen, across the Jordan. It was far from any settlement, from cities and from men. We wanted to be alone among the Arabs and the Beduin, to delve into the very heart of this wild country, the granary of Palestine, to build anew on the foundations Baron Rothschild had laid in 1885 and then destroyed. The villages of Horen beckoned to us, and we were not alone in our fascination. Every single agricultural worker in the country shared it.

Opposing the members with vision, were those who preached constancy, who urged us to stay where we were and looked on imagination as frivolous. Certainly it was heroic to conquer, to stand against Arab rifle fire and even perhaps to die. But real

heroism lay in facing the constant, day-to-day battle of creation—
the creation of workers, the creation of a self-supporting economy,
the transformation of the Jewish shopkeeper into a producer of
primary commodities. Yes, that was really heroic, they said. We
did not come to make war but to create a new homeland, to build
Hebrew villages which would live by what they produced, and to
make them prosper.

There were many more conflicts like this, while the urge to
create and put down roots worked strongly within us. Our hunger
for work and for the soil after thousands of years of exile over-
whelmed us. But we had fulfilment from our toil. Day by day we
saw with our own eyes how everything was growing, flowering and
developing.

The farmers of Galilee, our neighbours, observed us closely.
The younger ones sincerely hoped that our experiment would
succeed, while the older ones, deep in a rut, sneered at our efforts.
They had had experience, and knew in advance that we would
fail. Arabs worked in the Galilee settlements as in those of Judaea,
but here the difference was that the farmers themselves worked
with them, so that everyone progressed in the work together. They
were in a state of constant war against marauders and thieves, and
their relationship with the Arab workers who helped them in
defence and guard duties, was much better than was the case in
Judaea. The Judaean farmers had not yet learnt about the latest
idea, the kibbutz and its aims. We therefore had to prove our ability
to them, as well as convince ourselves of it. Despite the certainty
and faith that filled our hearts, we were sometimes assailed with
doubts. We had a difficult task to perform. Malaria still sapped our
strength and weakened our bodies; the work itself was by no means
easy. Our bodies wearied, our feet stumbled, our heads ached.
Our food was meagre and of poor quality, and the sun was pitilessly
hot and weakened us still more. These conditions caused many
thousands of Jews to leave the country, despairing of success.
Sometimes we ourselves faltered, but we stayed on, telling ourselves that this was all we had to cling to. We strove to the limit of
our strength and this striving gave us courage—and we won through.
A second year passed, one without losses, when we lived from the
yield of our work alone. The same workers who were looked down
on by the employers and who even doubted themselves sometimes,

c

were doing all the jobs on the farm—ploughing and sowing and harvesting. This was victory.

Poalei Zion, our political party and our newspaper, played a great part in our lives. They were our family, they examined our actions, watched us—and paid minute attention to our experiments. Our general requests and questions did not always get into print, but we took counsel with close friends in the party when we had troubles and problems which vexed us. There were cases of members leaving the kibbutz, but they were few and far between. One morning for instance, one of the founders of the kibbutz, Zvi Yehudah, left suddenly, bitterness in his heart. He went to Tiberias without having decided what to do next. There had been quarrels between him and the rest of the members. They said that he was a stubborn man and without humility. He became the instructor of the kibbutz at Hitin, a group of immigrants from Lodz in Poland. They did their agricultural training at Degania, but despite this our contacts were never more than tenuous.

Zvi was not the first to leave. Before him, one of the girls, also a founder member, had left as well. Sarah Malkin had been the mother of the commune. She had been the first girl member to obtain paid work, and when she came up to Kinneret to the settlement at Um-Juni, she was also the first to understand the duty of a woman in our settlement. From the very beginning she demanded the right to work in the garden and do all the other farming jobs, but she refused to do any housework. She demanded that more girls should be made members, but was refused. Apart from the objective consideration that the work was monotonous agricultural labour which it was impossible for girls to do, there was also a psychological, subjective consideration. The male members of the kibbutz did not understand her motives. She left and did not return, and her going caused sadness in our little band.

Our members were 18 to 25 years old. All their spiritual and bodily strength, all their will, all their energy, all their faith, were bent towards one goal—work!

The men worked with all their strength and managed to achieve a great deal. Our senior members, the founders, were always in the van when there was work to be done, and the newer members were thus impelled to work hard also, even though their experience and aptitude might be less. Some were negligent of course, and dropped their tools wherever they happened to be when work was over for the day. They were either never found, or else were broken and spoiled. Some people spent two years doing nothing but ploughing, but were still not competent when the third year came round. Others were willing, but spoiled things. However, they put them to rights, and worked hard.

Many members did not do any reading, not even a newspaper, and did not want to know what was going on in the world outside. 'What do I care about anything as long as I do my work well?' That was their attitude, and many of them never went outside Degania to the city from one year's end to the next.

On Saturday nights we used to gather at the 'office' to allocate the work. Some jobs were split up by the day, others by the week or the month. The watchman would change places with the yard man. The young girls who were new to the kibbutz would work in the kitchen under the supervision of one of the young men. Somebody would be detailed to clean out the rooms and repair our linen. A young girl would be sent to work in the plant nursery and vegetable garden. As time went by, some members of the kibbutz became proficient at all the jobs on the farm.

We were generally short of labour. In the summer we always had at least twenty per cent of our members ill, and sometimes the figure would be as high as fifty per cent. Sometimes there would be so few people available, that tasks would have to be shared out afresh. When the official allocation of jobs had been completed, there were still unofficial arrangements to be made and problems to face. Many of the really conscientious members used to sit up discussing them until the small hours.

In the winter, sowing was the main job. After our evening meal we would fill some sacks with seed and prepare the ploughs and other implements. We used to get up while it was still dark. The watchman would come in and light a candle in the room, and we would jump out of bed. A tour of guard duty lasted two weeks, and every watchman had his own way of waking us. Some would shout, 'Get up!', and disappear. Others would shake every one of us gently and say, 'Get up, get up. It's late.' Others, yet again, would not even come into the room, but would just bang loudly on the door without saying anything. Some watchmen used to fire their rifles, and we would leap up to see what was wrong.

25

When the kettle boiled we would drink tea, and between cups eat fresh bread and green olives. The watchman would recount the night's happenings; how he was supposed to have kept an eye on some dough that was rising, how he was to have made sure that the water did not boil over, how he was supposed to have woken the girls who worked in the kitchen—and how he had forgotten to do any of these things. Everybody would laugh, because the same sort of thing had happened to all of us.

Then we would get up one by one and go out to the yard, or the stables. The mules would recognise their drivers, who would brush and curry-comb them.

The yard emptied. Some members went out to the fields and a few remained behind to repair farm implements, clean out the cattle shed, or work in the vegetable garden. Only one or two of the young men were there to have breakfast with the girls. The yard man would grow angry because the girls kept him busy with house-work all the time.

In the fields, ploughing went on apace though it was hard going. At breakfast time, everyone gathered in a circle round a big pot of yoghourt. Someone distributed thick slices of bread and we all helped ourselves to the yoghourt. Ploughing continued, turning over the long furrows, one after the other.

At last evening came, and the yard filled with people again, all of them tired and covered in dust. Everybody went to wash and put on a clean white shirt. In the kitchen the floors had been scrubbed and all the girls were cleanly dressed. The tables were laid, the samovar, brought by one of our members all the way from Odessa, was boiling. Then the food was served and everyone began to eat and talk about the day's work. One of the members would note down in a book all that had been done and by whom. While we drank our tea the next day's work was apportioned.

Ploughing and sowing were winter jobs. Harvesting, cutting the grass, and hay-making were summer jobs and went on for three months. It was back-aching work in the blazing sun. Gnats and flies used to drive the mules crazy, flying into their eyes and ears, clustering under their bellies and under their tails, and stinging them cruelly. At last it was all finished, however, and everyone turned for home.

Threshing time approached. We had to hurry and start, because there was nothing left to feed the stock with and no flour for bread. We might have to sell some of our crop in advance, before prices had risen.

The piles of sheaves were always arranged in a particular pattern on the threshing floor, a specific distance apart, so that the wheat could be threshed separately from the barley. Before threshing started, we climbed up on to the stacks of sheaves, and lifted them up one by one, cutting the ties securing them. Then we spread them out ready for threshing, adding more next morning. Learners or hired youths from Tiberias were put in charge of the mules on the threshing sledge and the stone slabs where they trod out the grain, all day long. Once threshing began, it continued at tremendous tempo, some people making extra efforts, to compensate for others who could not stand the pace and fell ill or had to stop and rest.

And so our work continued, changing with the seasons—sowing, harvesting, threshing. Our spirits were high because our crops were giving excellent yields, and the land remained as rich as ever.

We had seen the well-established Galilee settlements, set up many years earlier, and the trees they had planted. So attractive was the sight, that we laid out avenues of trees even before we moved into our new houses. When the move had been completed, we started to make plans to extend the settlement's farming activities. We decided to plant 40 dunams of land with vines, almonds and olives, allocated a few dunams for vegetable growing, and considered planting a citrus grove. We also planned to buy some cows and calves in order to get the dairy side started. Of course there were many differences over these plans. Some members wanted the kibbutz to restrict itself to cereal crops and felt that we should not engage in new activities which no one else in the area had tried. We were still buying our eggs, vegetables, and sometimes even fruit from the surrounding villages or in Tiberias. We all knew that this was not the proper way of doing things, but despite this there were still members who did not want us to branch out.

The young girls and women were in favour of adding to the range of our activities, because they would be able to participate in them and so escape from housework, or from working in the kitchen or the laundry. They also wanted to bring more young women into the kibbutz. The controversy did not last long, but it made a deep impression on our group.

In the meantime the Arabs brought eggs, vegetables and fish on their donkeys. As time went on a Sephardi family called Menahem took over the task of supplying us with these commodities. Our small vegetable garden behind the kitchen yielded cucumbers in abundance, as well as carrots and radishes. We bought a few chicks to rear, but the experiment was unsuccessful. We had almost no eggs on the farm and Arab cows gave no milk in the summer, so our diet consisted mainly of vegetables of various kinds, soup and purées of different sorts. Eating so many oily things and drinking so much water (it was so hot at Degania in the summer that we were always at the taps in the shower-room) was not very good for our health. Everyone complained of some ailment or other—chronic indigestion, lack of energy, listlessness. The bread was very bad too, and we often threw it away. The meals were often burnt and we used to send the plates back to the kitchen, so many that we called it the railway, and said, 'Steam back to the kitchen with this'. Heaven knows how much distress and anger we must have caused the girls working in the kitchen. They used to cry bitterly when a meal was burnt, or the bread did not rise properly.

The fault did not lie with them, however, but with the lack of ingredients. At the beginning, of course, they did not know how to cook, and by the time a girl *had* learnt, she had spent so much time in the kitchen that she wanted a change of job. Since our food did not satisfy us, we used to go into the food store in the evenings or at night to make tea and eat bread. We would eat sugar or raisins with it, or dip it in oil. These habits led to chaos and waste.

Our daily diet affected our work, as is only natural. Forty names would be put down for work in the evening, but only fifteen people would appear, as the others would be too weak to get up. We asked for advice and received suggestions, but nothing seemed to help. The women, for their part, wanted to cut down their work in the kitchen and in the house as much as possible and work in the fields instead. Their argument ran as follows: 'You men go and work in the kitchen at non-creative jobs, and then perhaps you will begin to adopt a more respectful attitude towards cleanliness and tidiness, because you will know just what hard work it is keeping a place clean and tidy.' Their request was granted and men were sent to work in the kitchen, at first singly and then in pairs. The men did the heavy labouring jobs like raking out and stoking the stove, lifting heavy buckets and vats, scrubbing the pots and pans, swabbing the floors and chopping wood. The men also acted as mediators between the kitchen and the yard, and helped in the purchasing of supplies. The situation was hotly debated at our meeting. At first the men who put on aprons to wash dishes or swab the floor were jeered at, but gradually members got used to the idea and it became a custom.

In summer the climate was cruel. We were more than 600 feet below sea level and in time we became enfeebled from the heat. The hot season began at the end of April, with the heat growing more oppressive as the day wore on, and in the afternoon a hot wind would blow strongly. Our water was always warm and did not taste as if it came from the Jordan or Kinneret, and we were always very thirsty. Even the nights were hot and stifling. Inside the room it was difficult to fall asleep because of the stuffy atmosphere and our sweating, so we used to sleep in the open almost every night in the summer. Sometimes it was completely impossible to sleep, even in the open, no matter how tired we were after a day's work. Then there was nothing for it but to go and bathe in the Jordan and afterwards try again to get off to sleep. If it had not been for Kinneret and the Jordan it would have been impossible to live there.

Our working day was a long one in that climate, and as already mentioned, we were weak because of our miserable diet. We began to doubt whether it would be possible to bring all our plans to fruition in our steadily deteriorating state of health. We used to get up in the mornings, listless and tired, without any energy at all, with aching heads and feeble hands, and stumble drowsily along to our work after a scant meal of radishes in oil, and a drink of water. At noon we had a drink of water, and in the evening another meagre meal and more water. We used to doze off at table, waking up only when the stinging of the flies became so fierce that it was almost like being stung by a scorpion. Becoming impatient, some of us would start to sing or fool about to wake up the others and get back to work.

The winter was quite different—short and pleasant. There would be two months of rain and then three months of spring, the same sun that scorched us in summer shining gently and caressingly. The uncultivated fields would be covered with brightly-coloured wild flowers, while those already harrowed would be smooth and empty. There would be waves on Kinneret and the Jordan would flow faster. We used to mount mules or horses and ride into the river until the water reached our saddles, or sit in a boat tied to the horse's bridle with a length of rope, feeling the horse pulling with all its strength against the streaming current.

Mount Hermon in the distance was bright and beautiful, mantled in snow, while Safed looked down from the mountain tops and sparkled in the sun. We used to ride through the fields, our horses sleek and fresh, on the look-out for strange flocks and their shepherds, cantering or trotting as the fancy took us. When we arrived at the particular field we wanted to get to, we used to let the horses graze, while we climbed to the top of the watchman's hill which overlooked all the fields. Holding the horse's bridle, one could sit and read to one's heart's content.

And still work filled every cranny of our souls, for there was nothing else all day long, from two hours before dawn until after dark. We forgot the world outside and shut ourselves inside the smaller world of our settlement, wiping out our memories of the past. This was what we thirsted for constantly, the spring that refreshed us and gave tranquillity to our souls—the knowledge that we were working out new lives for ourselves. We treasured it, though the way was hard. But there was one question which troubled us constantly—whether we ought to give ourselves over completely to that particular way of life; whether we ought to cut ourselves off from all sources of culture and spiritual inspiration. Nevertheless, it was clear that we could not triumph over ourselves in any other way. We wanted to be the tillers of the soil, and this demanded devotion—to the soil itself, to work, animals, plants and implements.

But we could not remain completely isolated, nor did we wish to. Members of the kibbutz could always be seen, at mealtimes, during rest periods, after work, on Saturdays and when they were not well (and so not working), with books open before them. We read and read. Reading become an obsession, and there were some who prayed that they could fall ill and so manage to read a little more. There were some individuals, however, who did not find pleasure in reading. In the evenings they used to sit and talk about work, the mules, what had been planted, and similar subjects, and they jeered at the intelligentsia and their books.

The bright city across the lake beckoned to us, with its theatres and its art, its diversions and its cultural life, and we yearned for them all. It was almost as if they would tear us away from the soil where we had only managed as yet to put down the flimsiest of roots.

And Saturday—that was our day of rest. There was already a feeling of Sabbath on Friday evening. The dining hall was spotless and the lamps were reflected in the freshly swabbed floor. The cloths on the tables added a festive air, and the Sabbath meal was something special—fish from the Jordan, pancakes and tea. We would sing with sheer joy, and then dancing would begin. On Saturday morning, the only people who got up early were those whose turn it was to lay the tables for breakfast—tea and two cakes—and those who had to clean out the room, swill out the stables, and feed and water the animals. Then visitors would start arriving. Girls would call to us from the other side of the river, asking us to take them across. If the member on duty could not find a volunteer to help him, he would have to spend the whole day taking guests back and forth.

One of the mules, Zipora, was so intelligent that she would ford the river, taking someone over to the other side on her back, and then return to the yard unaccompanied, and of her own free will. Because of her intelligence, Zipora was in demand for other duties as well. She was not frightened by gun shots, so she was a regular mount for watchmen on patrol. Her other duty was to pump water. We would cover her head and eyes with a sack and tie a pole across her shoulders, connecting it with strong wires to the pump wheel, and she would walk round and round, turning the wheel without supervision and without changing her tempo. When the small water tank on the roof overflowed on to the balcony, the girls would shout to the yard man who ran over and took the sack off Zipora's head, and she would stop her steady walking round and round.

The rest of the members, those not on duty, would not linger too much in their beds on Saturday, so as to make the day of rest longer and to be able to enjoy it properly. Some wrote letters, others went for walks to nearby villages and settlements.

After the midday meal came the general meeting of kibbutz members in one of the living rooms. Everyone was very serious-minded about things and we did not find it too difficult to solve our economic problems. But our social problems were more intractable. What sort of cultural life ought we to have? How should children be brought up in a kibbutz (and this before there was even one child in the kibbutz)? From these questions we went on to consider such topics as bringing new girl members into the kibbutz, whether we needed more workers, and so on.

At one general meeting we decided to institute a suggestions book in which members could write down their suggestions for remedying any defects in our communal life, or put forward some new proposal or plan. The book was prepared and some members did write in it at first, but the project petered out. We had thought that some members who found it difficult to speak in public would find it easier to make written suggestions, but apparently they were as loath to use their pens as their tongues.

Our members continued to progress and acquire more skill in their chosen jobs on the farm. As with any group, some were independent and of strong character, others weak and easily influenced. The former were very active in economic and social matters, the latter hardly at all. There were many different approaches to affairs in the kibbutz and things were not always done the way the majority wanted them to be done. This very often led to covert murmurings and then open complaints, and these in their turn often led to quarrels. If allowed to continue unchecked, this kind of behaviour would have endangered the entire life and peace of our community. The only possible solution was to cultivate a spirit of give and take.

We had to stop stressing our differences until we knew everything about each other—our desires and inclinations, our good and bad points, our private as well as our public faces. In this way mutual respect could grow, and so could social concord. We could round out our society then, living in peace as one family.

Many members did give in to each other in such material matters as food, living quarters, clothes, and so on. It was a different story where economic questions were concerned. The approach of members was in many cases highly individual. Controversies multiplied, not just about general farming and economic matters, but about day-to-day work, for this was our life and our whole moral code. We had put our entire souls into it, as writers and painters put their souls into *their* creations.

There were many conflicts and many adversaries, because the kibbutz, and everything to do with it, filled our lives. The original members, those who had belonged to the commune at Hadera, formed a kind of special group on their own. They bore the burden of work and affairs, and mostly discussed matters among themselves, since they all shared the same room. The rest of the members would not surrender their right to participate in economic and social affairs and exert their influence. Often their ideas were different from those of the commune and its supporters, and each group would hold separate consultations. At the end they came together to thrash matters out.

The commune said, 'You can run things if you want to. Just say what is to be done and we shall do it'. The others said that they did not want to run things, but just wanted to be on the inside of affairs. The commune replied that they had not deliberately set out to control everything, but that the present state of affairs had come about of its own volition. The others replied that things would have to change, because otherwise there would always be two factions in the kibbutz, obviously an undesirable development.

It was clear that the commune would have to loosen its grip on kibbutz matters, though this would not be easy. The rebels consulted among themselves and nominated one of their number to put their demands—that the commune should relinquish the treasurership, the making out of the daily work lists and various other official duties. This destroyed the feeling of intimacy among the kibbutz members for a time, and some of the members were no longer on speaking terms with each other.

However, later on the whole affair died down, and indeed it turned out to have been a blessing. The older members drew closer to the newer ones and the kibbutz became a unified whole, from the founder members to those who had been there only a year, although the clash had made a lasting impression on the older and more active members. They had maintained comradely relations throughout the whole affair, and their attitude had been free from jealousy or pettiness. Nevertheless, when two members of the commune left the kibbutz at the beginning of its third year, we felt that this was a dangerous portent. From then on we received frequent letters from members who were ready to leave if this would lead to general peace in the kibbutz, but almost everyone felt that this was not the way. To leave solved nothing; we had to grow up and learn to live together in our chosen way of life. This was a difficult period for victors and vanquished alike. Many meetings were held when the participants laid bare their innermost hearts and made public confessions.

Those who lingered in the kitchen on Saturdays and at night were causing increasing waste of groceries and provisions. Although our scanty diet was insufficient, this eating round the stove was disorganising the kitchen and threatening hygiene. It also angered the women who worked in the kitchen, because it made them late in preparing breakfast.

One evening, the provision store was found to be under lock and key. So was the bread. What was this, the bread and provisions locked up? The hungry ones would have to stay hungry! Could this really be happening? It was enough to make an honest member think of leaving! The air was full of explanations and self-justification and then the atmosphere returned to normal.

It has already been mentioned that our young lives were not free from self-criticism or indeed from more general criticism. These hidden thoughts found free expression in the notes and letters which members often sent each other for what they considered to be worthwhile reasons, and this habit had become an integral part of our lives.

It was night-time and the sky was powdered with stars. The young men were sitting on the steps of the new stone-built house, singing to the accompaniment of a guitar, when all at once they felt hungry. The midday meal had been sent back by 'railway,' and the bread had not been properly baked. Some of them got up, broke the kitchen lock and satisfied their hunger. The next morning the girls found that what they had laboriously prepared for breakfast had already been eaten and they were very angry. There was a crisis, followed by an exchange of notes.

'My dear Yosef,

I love Degania and have a high regard for you. Since my behaviour has apparently resulted in your wanting to leave, I wish to inform you openly and with the utmost sincerity, that if I am indeed the cause of your wishing to leave, I am prepared to go away from Degania. Everything is upside down and I do not know where I stand. Please tell me straight away, and I will do what I have to do.

Yours

S. Dayan.'

The reply was not long delayed:

'You and others are together the cause of our leaving Degania, but if you all left, this would still not impel us to remain. If you were to leave it would ruin everything. It is better that Miriam and I should leave Degania and then you will not feel as you have done up till now.

Yosef Baratz.'

These exchanges took place on the impulse of the moment. In the event, of course, nobody left.

Some of our members were convinced vegetarians, and although they changed their way of life radically when they joined the kibbutz, they did not relinquish their convictions in this respect. It was difficult for the girls to prepare special food for them, for although the rest of us lived on a mainly vegetarian diet, we ate a great deal of fish, especially salt herring. The vegetarians wanted to have their own special table, but were unsuccessful in this.

There were endless discussions on the subject. What would the vegetarians do, it was asked, when their cow grew old? Would they slaughter it or wait for it to die of old age? And what would they do with its calf? Rear it at a loss or slaughter it? And what if, when the eggs hatched, they turned out to be cocks and not hens, would not the vegetarians sell them for killing? The questions flew back and forth.

Strangely enough, it was the vegetarians who were hardest on the work animals, beating them until they drew blood. When we commented on this in astonishment, they replied: 'It is beyond our strength to alter life's cruelty. Are you going to scoff at us because we aspire not to do evil or shed blood, and do not succeed?'

Some of the first boys to complete their studies at the secondary school in Jaffa came to Degania to work and learn the various farming jobs. We welcomed them to the kibbutz and drew them into our life. We regarded them as the vanguard, the forerunners of many other boys, who on leaving school would exchange their books for work and the study of nature. But only a few came after them, and they did not stay long. After a year, they left Degania and agricultural work.

Many other people came to us for agricultural training, even from abroad. They had heard of Degania and it was for them an example of free and unrestricted living where a man could fulfil himself. The farm was open to all, for we needed working hands. We thought that our guests would adapt themselves and be able to render really effective assistance, but most of them disappointed us. So many of them were superficial and unused to communal life. They used to interfere in matters they knew nothing about and hamper progress. Others were natural buffoons and clowns. There was the man who shouted 'Fire, fire!' when he saw smoke coming from the kitchen; the man who thought that we were being attacked by thieves every time someone fired a rifle; the one who wanted to make sweeping changes in the schedule of work the first week he came. The girls also varied. One day, two came and immediately made a place for themselves in the hearts of everyone in the kibbutz. Their previous life had been altogether different; they had not even heard of Zionism. When they came they brought a new spirit with them, and all the members were jolted out of their rut. They became bound up with love, beauty, literature.

The girls stayed on with us and our simple, fundamental life captivated their young hearts. One of them stayed for many years and brought good taste and culture to many different aspects of our lives, especially in the education of our children later on, although still suffering because of the experiences of her earlier life.

Times were hard for young people in reactionary Russia in those days, after the failure of the revolution. There was no inspiration for Jewish youth. When the Balkan War broke out and Bulgaria was involved, this young girl wanted to devote herself to nursing the war-wounded, so she ran away from home to Sofia. However, she soon returned, having taken pity on the old folks who had brought her up and looked after her with so much trouble. But she did not know whether she had made the right choice. She spent all her time looking at the books which filled her father's bookcase. They were in Hebrew, which she could not even read. They reminded her of the country her father often spoke about with longing. Then with surprise, she realised that they showed her the path she should follow. She packed a few belongings, travelled to Odessa, took passage in a cargo ship and finally reached Haifa. She went to Merhavia and worked there. When she had earned enough to pay her fare, she took the train to Degania, and there she stayed.

Her wise words spread joy all around, but her heart was sad. By day she worked, showed a cheerful face to the outside world, joked and talked, but in the evening she made haste to get away on her own. She did not eat with us in any case, but went out into the fields and relived her past life in her imagination. She thought about the city and the university, about her studies, about books and the theatre, about the old professor who had treated her like one of his own children. Should she strike roots here, or should she move on? Oppressed by these thoughts, she wandered about the fields of Degania, and perhaps she shed a few tears sometimes under the stars. Her decision was to stay.

Whenever family questions came up, educational problems, whether we ought to have private living quarters and kitchens, and so on, we always discussed them at our general meetings. At one meeting a member stood up and proposed that any kibbutz member who wished to marry ought to wait for five years from the time the kibbutz had become established on a sound basis, and its members properly integrated. Not many months later the proposer himself became the first man among us to take a wife.

And the wedding itself was no simple matter, either. Should it be a religious one with all the ceremony? The would-be bride and groom did not know themselves. There was no need for any ceremony, but on the other hand, why dispense with a custom which adds something special to the memory of a special occasion? Other members made fun of them. 'Just look at these revolutionaries! They want to keep things just as they were, with marriage lines, a ring, and all the rest of the trappings.'

Friday dawned, fine and mild, and everyone was cheerful and smiling. In the yard preparations for the wedding went forward.

The sweeper on duty cleaned up, sweeping up great heaps of muck which were loaded on to a cart and taken off to the manure heap. One of our comrades picked some flowers and shrubs and decorated the walls of the dining hall. Early in the morning we had sent out two carts, one to Tiberias to bring back wine, almonds and fruit, and the other to Milhamia to fetch the shochet to perform the wedding ceremony. The driver of the second cart was, incidentally, an impassioned opponent of all religious ceremonies.

The kitchen girls were busy with their preparations. Aprons flying, they hurried from the kitchen to the store-room and back again to the kitchen. One of the men swabbed the floor and kept the stove going. Work in the fields stopped in the afternoon, and the ploughmen came back to the farm, riding on their mules. The carts were lined up in a row, and all the implements and tools stood against the wall in the yard. Everybody rushed off to shave and change into Sabbath clothes. A member was found to write the marriage certificate, two more to witness it, and then the shochet arrived. We all gathered together and made our way slowly to the banks of the Jordan, where we put up the wedding canopy. The shochet conducted the ceremony and then we all returned to the brightly lit dining hall. A meal had been spread and there were some bottles of wine on the tables. Tall candles gave added light and increased the festive spirit and charm of the occasion.

And the young girl? Nobody had seen her all day. She was shut up in her room sewing her wedding dress. She shed many tears as she worked, tears of longing for her mother. But when she came out in her white wedding gown she carried herself proudly, with her hair in two long, fine plaits down her back. She stepped lightly into the dining hall, and without sitting down, raised her glass and was then drawn into the circle of dancers. After dancing nine complete rounds without a stop, she let go her companions' hands and burst into the centre of the circle, alone. Her dancing began quietly and grew ever more stormy. Her comrades drew back and made the circle bigger, singing and clapping their hands in accompaniment to the dancing of this young girl who had found where she belonged after many wanderings and tribulations. Then they came together again and danced in a circle, moving hands and feet in unison, with speed and precision.

Dancing went on late into the night, and then some guests came over from Kinneret. We drank wine and ate almonds and walnuts. We talked about crop rotation, the market for vegetables in Damascus, the irrigation of bean plants, the best way of pumping water from Kinneret. This was talking shop with a vengeance, but we enjoyed it. It did not seem incongruous to us on such an occasion.

The first child in the kibbutz was born to Miriam Ostrovsky-Baratz, one of its founders. She was a country girl, happy and gay, healthy, and one of the strongest in the group, able to do the hardest jobs. Her happy disposition had a good effect on everyone, and in our Petach Tikva days, days of hunger and dejection, we had only to hear singing and dancing on the road to Ein Ganim or on the outskirts of the settlement, to know that she was at the head of a procession of unemployed who were looking for work. With her comrades from the commune she came to Um-Juni and later to Degania. Her companions failed to stay the course for various reasons and left the kibbutz, but she stayed on, going from strength to strength. She had carved out a special place for herself among the members.

She gave birth to her child in the Tiberias hospital. The baby's father was in Merhavia at the time, having gone there after the murder of one of its members, to help strengthen the guard against the Arabs of the Jezreel Valley, who were casting covetous glances at the settlement.

Despite Miriam's attachment to the kibbutz, her readiness to follow the will of the majority, and her years of training, when it came to the point she did not find it easy to put into practice what she had been taught to believe.

She set up a private kitchen for herself and started to lead her own private life. After the long working day the parents wanted to be with their child, and the only time they could be with him was in the evening when work was over. This was a tremendous blow to the kibbutz and its ideology. Members who spent their hours of rest apart from their comrades were cut off from the most important affairs. It was during these hours that working arrangements were made, plans prepared for the farm, economic and social matters discussed. And the shame of it! To abandon without any effort to maintain it the code that had been talked about for years, when the birth of a child in the kibbutz had still been in the future.

D

After all, this was the very foundation of the kibbutz. The family, the child—this was the first thread in the fabric of our new society! When the child was born all the members had said, 'A son has been born to Degania', and in their dreams of the future great hopes were born. Who knew what mighty happenings this youngster might bring in his train? Was this to be the end of the dream?

There were coaxings and cajolery, mutual reproofs and reconciliations, exhortations, and consultations, until the breach was healed and the whole incident forgotten. Then happiness reigned in the kibbutz family abode.

Even though there was as yet only one child, the question of how children should be brought up was frequently discussed. It had originally been raised some time before, because in our ardent society all sorts of things were talked about long before they happened. The people who had most to say on this particular subject were the bachelors. All the kibbutz members talked as if they were mothers and fathers of long standing. They discussed the subject without really knowing much about it, considering it from the point of view of freeing the mother for work on the farm. The mother was to be freed from the tyranny of bringing up and looking after children, thus becoming free to work. For to be a working woman was the ideal!

To be a working mother was to be saved from idleness, which led to gossip and petty-mindedness. A woman must work like a man and play an active part in life. We did not know how this could be done and continued our search for a solution. Perhaps a creche was the answer, like those organised for workers' children in various other counties. If a mother worked in a factory she could leave her child at the creche, and it would be looked after until the evening when the mother returned from work. But would it be a good thing for us to take a child away from its parents and deprive it of the loving regard of its father and mother? In factories abroad there was no alternative, but could we do the same in order to give a woman independence?

Miriam's devotion to her work in the cowshed would not let her spend all her time looking after her son. She would put him down in one of the stalls, and regardless of the flies crawling all over his face, she would get on with her milking, singing at her work. The second mother, Devora my wife, never managed to spend enough time with our child Moshe somehow, and as a result he got trachoma. A solution had to be found. It may be amusing to reproduce here some minutes of a discussion of this problem, which have survived from those days.

Yosef Bussel: Looking after children is not the mother's duty only, but that of all the women. The main consideration in everything we do must be the principle of co-operation. Everything must be public knowledge, because if things are kept private they interfere with work. As far as the pay for looking after children is concerned, there is no doubt that it must be provided by all of us, because in communal living all expenses must be shared. It is impossible for people not to pay their share because they themselves have no children. In fact all the outlay connected with bringing up and caring for children must be shared.

Devora Dayan: Of course children must be looked after, but the right person must be found for the job. If none of the women here can do it, we must bring in somebody from outside the kibbutz. We must also decide how much time the mother herself needs to spend with her child in order to look after it. Only then will it be possible to leave the child with a nursemaid, and for that job a woman from outside would be better. In the first place she will be more conscientious because she will probably not want to work on the farm; in the second place nobody here can do the job, mainly because so few know Hebrew.

Yosef Bussel: I suggest that in order to be able to pay for a nursemaid, we dismiss Ben-Yehuda. (He meant Dr. Baruch Ben-Yehuda, the Principal of the Herzlia secondary school, who was giving us Hebrew lessons in the evenings.)

Sonia Meron-Bloch: We need a teacher just as much as we need a nursemaid. And if we do get a nursemaid, it is better to get one with qualifications.

Yosef Baratz: Since there are children of varying ages, and one of them is already old enough to start lessons, we need a nursemaid who can also be a teacher, since we cannot afford both.

Yosef Bussel had established the principle of joint coverage of expenses. Devora Dayan stressed what a responsible job the education of children was, and pressed for the appointment of a qualified person from outside the kibbutz, since not one of the women members knew Hebrew. She also declared that a child should stay in the care of its mother for at least one year.

The discussion was abandoned, but it had cleared the air and helped to avoid many dissensions later on, when the question of how to educate our first children became even more complex. Our discussion also served to highlight another question: Could grown-ups educate each other? Self-education had been the creed of our great comrade and teacher, A. D. Gordon. But who could try to follow in his footsteps and not fail? It needed great strength of character to be able to examine oneself, daily, questioning everything one had done. What good have I done? What evil have I done? What must I put right? How can I improve myself? By asking himself all these questions, and educating himself, a man could save his soul. If everybody were to see his own failings and rectify them, a just and honest society would evolve. The relationship between individuals, between man and man, man and society, man and woman, man and child even, would change entirely.

Youngsters of twenty to twenty-five, we had wandered to this desolate spot from across the sea, and here we were without parents and without children. There were no grandparents, no father or mother here to turn to for help or advice. We were proud, and shut out parents and grandparents from our hearts, speaking slightingly of them because they seemed to be so old and did not understand.

One of our members, Yosef Bussel, had a mother in Palestine, but we would not let her live with her son at Degania. She was forced to live in Tiberias in a small, stuffy room together with her daughter, who worked as a seamstress to support her. This sister of Yosef's was dumb, but was able to express herself by making signs with her hands. She came to Degania every day to do sewing, and every evening returned to Tiberias to her old mother.

Up till now I have not managed to embark on the unforgettable chapter of youthful love that unfolded while we were building up the kibbutz and establishing it on a firm foundation. There are only hints in the extracts which follow. These are letters of longing written when we were separated because of illness or when one of us had to make a journey. Some letters are quoted in full. They and the extracts form a continuous link with those far-off days, when they were a part of the very fabric of our lives.

In 1913 I was at Merhavia, helping to guard the fields, because the watchmen of the settlement needed reinforcements. I wrote:

'I was sad to learn from your letter of the sorry physical and spiritual state of Degania. The young women are ill and so are some of the young men. Some have gone away. Who is left? And what about the harvest and the rest of the work? Especially when there is nobody to work in the kitchen. I wish I could be with you now at Degania, but here I am a soldier and must stay at my post.'

And later:

'So the first boy has been born at Degania! What will Fate bring in his train? They should call him Adam, a name as exalted as our aspirations. For all of us I wish that our lives may lead us along the path we pray for in our hearts . . . From today Degania will begin to live the life of discipline that the prophets foretold in their visions. May we be purified from the taint of our days of exile and our spirits exalted. "Rejoice and be glad—for I am with you".'

Again:

'I am not well and am in Tiberias. At Merhavia the nights were beautiful, and the moon seemed different. On guard at night we looked on death and meditated on life. One night while I was on guard, Mirka Hazanowitz was killed, and we buried him in the morning. For the next few nights it seemed to me as if Mirka was riding up and down before my eyes, a kefiyeh on his head, his rifle on his shoulder, smiling his enchanting smile. We built a kind of hillock on his grave at Merhavia so that it will stand out.'

These words, written from the heart, were meant for a special recipient, that same young girl who came to Degania from Russia, and through our struggle to establish Degania on a firm basis, found in me her comrade. In our letters to each other, and in the notes exchanged between the members of the kibbutz, our joys and our sorrows, all the ferment of feeling and emotion in the kibbutz, found expression and were given full rein.

'Devora', I wrote, 'I have read your letter several times and it seems to me that I have understood it aright. Nevertheless, I must ask you what it all means and what led you to write to me and tell me all these things. I know that our backgrounds are different, and that you have a great store of knowledge of all kinds. Can someone who loves art and books succeed in life with a youngster who has had to work for a living from his early years and has had no time to study? Perhaps that will be the very factor that will smooth your path with me. Not very long ago, when I first began to admire and respect you—your personality, your life, your thoughts—I besought you to tell me all about them. I wanted to feel your emotions, to understand your thoughts and to know about your life. And you told me. I listened eagerly to your every word. Your tale was a part of your soul, and today it is a part of mine also. I find you enchanting, both as a woman and as a person'.

To one of our comrades I wrote:

'When we were young we remembered only our general life, our communal activities, and they gave us strength, raised our hopes and helped us to continue with our chosen way of life. Did we find that reality had not lived up to our dreams? Did we feel betrayed? Did we feel that we had spent all our youth in achieving our way of life? Whatever the reason, every one of us began to be concerned with his own personal joys and sorrows. This brought discord, anger and envy to the kibbutz.

'Our work has been crowned with success. The farm is well-ordered and thriving; the storehouse is richly stocked; our profits are calculated with enthusiasm and alertness; everyone takes pleasure in the situation. Nevertheless, morale is lower than it has ever been. People don't look at each other; their faces are expressionless and withdrawn; they very rarely say anything that comes from the heart. That is how things are now. Why?

'This week I wanted to see the doctor at Yamah (Yavniel), because I felt very weak. Several others wanted to come as well, so I harnessed Dov and Sarah to the cart and we all set off. When we set out on the return journey, darkness had already fallen. As we rode up the mountain, a dim light glimmered from Degania, hidden among the bends of the Jordan. As I looked at the light, my heart grew heavy within me and I asked myself the same question: "Why are things like this?" The full moon rose above the hills, and its beams kissed the calm waters of Kinneret. Its silvery light was reflected in the lake and made the night as bright as day. The mules trotted briskly down the mountainside and the wheels turned smoothly and fast. All around was peace and the very rocks seemed to be at rest. But when I came into the dining-hall and saw all the angry faces, my spirits sank . . .

'There is a great deal of work to do and only a few of us to do it. The mules, the donkeys, the horses, the cows and the calves are in very good condition. Zalah has calved, and Shehorah's calf has died. We have killed the ducks, and the broody hens have hatched about a hundred chicks. In field number 8 we have already ploughed some 200 dunams and in number 7 we have ploughed the rest as far as the Um-Juni road. The threshing is almost finished and practically all the barley is in store. The wheat should amount to about 105 metric tons, and there are another 68 or so metric tons to be weighed. This should earn us 4,000 francs profit. Provided we do not lose any more working hands, we should finish storing the grain in a month. The plantations are coming on quite well, considering the climate and conditions, but the watermelons have been a failure. We left the chick peas in the ground because there was nothing to pick. We have plenty of milk. Parcha and Brajinsky have been giving the best yields. When are you coming?'

In another letter, I wrote:

'Dear Yeruham,

'Life is full, and rich and colourful, but the people, oh the people! They quibble over every tiny detail, and the pleasure has gone out of things. Tanchum does not seem to be sensitive to the decline in enthusiasm. He is untouched by it, being a stranger to doubt and disillusionment and seeing only the positive, not the negative, aspect of everything. But we can feel it. Do you remember that evening when we spoke about the difference between the harvesting work this year and last year?

'Perhaps I should not have written to you about the negative side of our working life. I ought to have told you about the positive side instead, but that is how things are. We have just had our yearly celebration in honour of Herzl. It was a day when each of us remembered this outstanding personality, and his memory became greener, and pulsed within our minds. But the ceremony of remembrance in the Gan Herzl was banal and unedifying. What was worse, the mass of ordinary people, the workers of Galilee, forgot all about Herzl. Yes, they forgot all about him, even though it was they who began the custom of making the 20th of Tammuz a holiday, and holding a gathering by Kinneret on Jewish National Fund land. This time they danced and enjoyed themselves as if this were just an ordinary day off, another opportunity to dance and drink.

'What can I tell you about life at Degania? Most of the time we are working, and our limited free time is not really satisfying. Everyone is withdrawn and distant, concerned only with his own feelings and problems.

'I know that your life is also not free from sorrow and yearning, my dear friend, but there is a significance to it. If you suffer, it is a sign that your life is a beautiful one and full of import. As for Devora and me, well she has changed very much. She anticipated Degania's shortcomings.

'Shalom to you, and if you send me short letters, my replies will be no longer.

Yours, Shmuel.'

The rest of the letters quoted here were all written to Devora, his wife, who had gone to Sedjera because the kibbutz had decided that they could 'no longer consider her as a working partner'. Devora was in no physical condition to do the amount of work demanded, and she had had to leave.

She tried her best, but while a few years later, and today, a kibbutz could afford to have members whose agricultural productivity was below average, things were different then.

All the jobs demanded great physical strength and people like Devora, who could not stand the pace, were considered a burden, and if they stayed, felt guilty and unhappy.

Devora came from a different background . . .

The banks of the Dnieper—a great and mighty river which carried passenger ships, cargo ships, sailing ships, fishing vessels and rafts of timber from the forests for weeks and even months until they arrived at their destination—Prokhorovka. Prokhorovka was a sizeable township of several thousand peasant families, among them some Jewish families.

On the river bank stood a large house and next to it the small dwelling of the watchmen and servants. It was a sort of estate near the river, standing a little away from the town. And the Dnieper flowed by, its waters green and sparkling in the summer, but frozen solid in winter.

The whole river froze in winter, and traffic ceased. The estate was cut off as well. In the spring came the thaw and the big house by the river came to life again. In the yards were stacks of timber ready for sale to the merchants.

Devora's father, Yehiel Ze'ev Zatolovsky, was a trusted employee in charge of the timber stores. In the summer he bought up whole forests. Lumberjacks felled the trees, and then the timber was floated in rafts down the Dnieper to Prokhorovka, where it was sawn up ready for sale. Yehiel Ze'ev, the son of Rabbi Emmanuel, was a great scholar and one of the Hovevei Zion (Lovers of Zion) and he was extremely well-read. He had a wonderful library of books in Hebrew and Russian, and all the periodicals could be found at his house.

In the winter he used to sit on the sofa and warm himself by the stove, with plenty of books and newspapers and the telephone close at hand. He used to hold long conversations on the telephone with Zionists and people interested in the Hebrew language, and also with the non-Jewish intellectuals of the district—the priest, the doctor and government officials. Sometimes he would play cards, or chat with friends over a drink and doughnuts dipped in butter, or go sleigh-riding in the thick snow.

Devora's mother, Masha (Miriam), was born a country girl. She was good-hearted, patient and quiet. Her speech was slow and gentle, and a smile was never far from her lips and eyes. She busied herself in the house, and nothing ever fussed her or put her out. In the summer the house was always full of guests—friends of the children, businessmen, relatives—who had come to enjoy the summer scene, and she looked after them all.

There were three children, Devora (Varossia) who was the eldest, Yehoshua (Yeshike) and Ronia (Rachel) the child of their old age. The three of them studied in the neighbouring town, although Yehoshua sometimes came home to prepare for exams.

Devora was a youngster of six when she first started school in the town. She went on her own, muffled in a fur coat in the winter. She was the only Jewish girl among scores of non-Jewish children. The teacher was a priest with a cross on a chain round his neck, and the official language of the school was Ukrainian. In the distance could be seen the statue of Schevtschenko, the Ukrainian poet, while all around were fields and forests, and villages with their great herds of cattle, pigs and horses, and their fruit trees. Over them all reigned the River Dnieper.

All this made a deep impression on the little girl, who became steeped in the songs, the literature, the customs and the traditions of the Ukrainian countryside where she grew up.

When Devora grew older she went to a secondary school in Poltava, and in order to save her parents some of the expense involved, she started giving lessons to backward students. She continued to do this in Kiev too, when she eventually went on to study at the University there.

She was good at her lessons, and popular with her teachers. One of her professors, a Ukrainian called Rossoff, gave her research work to do. She had to investigate the measures being taken against malaria in the villages, and often led groups of teachers and students on visits to the Caucasus and other places. She passed all her examinations except the finals.

The years brought change and then revolution in Russia. Socialist parties were founded. The best writers, with Tolstoy at their head, analysed the Czarist regime and wrote about its short-comings. A constitution was proclaimed, the Duma was set up and then dissolved. The spiritual climate was one of rebellion, and Devora did what she could to help the sons of the people. She lectured at the evening institute and served food to hungry youths.

Then she returned home, to the big house with its spacious rooms. There was her father's room, its many bookcases crammed with books of poetry and prose, Jewish and non-Jewish. But she was not attracted by them. She was drawn to the Slav culture of the people among whom she lived. When the Balkan War broke out in 1912, she volunteered to go to the Bulgarian front as a nurse. It was then that doubt came upon her, suddenly. 'Where is my people? I do not know my people!' It was a time of crisis for her, and she found no answer to the question in her heart. She returned home and after a while began to look through the books and period-icals in her father's room. There she found her answer—Palestine, the homeland of her people, was her homeland too.

Without telling her parents where she was travelling to she set out secretly for the (to her) unknown land of Palestine. She did not want her parents to know she was leaving the Ukraine for Palestine, because they might have tried to stop her and there would have been arguments. Instead, they heard the news when she had already left, and it came as a tremendous shock.

Devora, twenty-one years old, was the only girl among the ten elderly Jews and the Slavs on the ship, making a pilgrimage to Jerusalem, the Holy City. The few coppers she had were enough to pay for a night's lodging at the workers' hostel in Haifa. She had one aim: to work in the fields of Palestine, wiping out her past life, the books and the lessons. For real life was in the daily struggle for bread.

One day in the spring of 1913 she set out from Zemach station for Eyta, wearing a long grey coat, and with her belongings in a basket. She went up on to the dining-hall balcony and looked tiredly around her, but there was nobody to meet her. She was a stranger. However, the letter of introduction she brought with her broke the ice and she became the guest of Israel Bloch. Everyone plied her with questions about Russia and Russian Jews. What was it like there? How were the Jews faring? And the young people? Would the Zionists among them come to Palestine? What new book had appeared? Then she was put to work at kneading a tub of dough.

The sweat poured from her and the flies were a torment. Her legs were tired with standing and her hands ached from kneading the dough. Everything seemed to be unsteady. But she persevered, and the dough rose and was baked and became bread. She was within reach of her life's goal—she was a worker!

At that time the kibbutz had determined to bend all their efforts towards evolving a different way of life from the usual one. They were going to live in a society imbued with one idea—that of working on the land and living a communal life. It was to be a closed society and its only contact with the outside world would be through an elected representative.

Guests came and went, but one day a guest came who brought with her ideas from a world we had forgotten—the world of the mind and the spirit. In her room could be heard conversations about literature, poetry, books, painting and art, the latest scient-ific discoveries, the value of beauty in human life, good taste in clothes, and good manners in social intercourse.

Kibbutz members clustered round her, wanting to breathe this atmosphere of culture and escape from the routine of work. They were attracted by her charm, her intelligence and her cultivated mind. She had a keen sense of perception, and the girls of the kibbutz reacted with anger and resentment. She was taken off kitchen work, but there was no other work for women as yet. Then a solution was found.

Two Sephardi women from Zemach, Parcha and Rosa, used to winnow out the last ears of grain from the coarse straw left after threshing, and Devora was sent to work with them. She filled the big sieve with straw, supported it at waist level on a short pole and twirled it round. The seeds fell through the mesh on to the ground and were then swept together and picked up. That was how Devora started doing farm work and achieved deliverance from working in the kitchen and from housework.

But she still knew nothing about the life and aims of the kibbutz. Even the language was strange to her, and she was as yet untried in physical labour. One of the girls said to her: 'Live with us and like us. This is a new life in a new-old land, and we want to possess our homeland physically and spiritally.'

When the grain had all been stored, Devora went to Sedjera to learn Hebrew from Jachanowitz (Yachnai), a very good teacher. In her heart she loved Degania and its members and she tried to understand what it was that was making her integration into kibbutz life so difficult. Devora dreamed of doing educational literary work and she was right to prepare herself for it. Unfortunately, few were the members who understood it or were prepared to look so far ahead, and we were separated for a while—letters being the only contact.

She wrote to me, among other things:

'I still feel a great love for Degania. Why did they not understand me, and why did I reveal all my doubts and disappointments to them? I came to them and said: "I belonged to a different life and perhaps you look askance at it, but it may be that I did not find truth there and came to find it with you. I want to share in your dedication". But they rejected me, and then I suffered.'

In my reply I tried to offer consolation:

'I came back from work happy, because I knew I had someone to discuss things with, to exchange opinions and share feelings. Things are better for me now than they were last year, and though they are not so good for you now, my dear, they will change. The initial difficulties will pass and you will be able to enjoy the life of independence before you, particularly once you have learnt

Hebrew. I was happy to hear that you are making such good progress with the language.

'Life at Degania is not easy now, because I somehow feel considerably less sociable and less willing to take part in organised communal life. If anyone had told me two years ago that a young girl could bring about such changes in me, I would have thought him crazy. Now, as I follow the plough, my imagination runs riot and I can see us both in Kiev or Prokhorovka, or even California. If Degania makes 15,000 francs next year we shall have the means to go to California, "the Grand Tour" as you call it.

'Yesterday, after Tanchum had asked to be sent away from the kibbutz, I felt that I ought to give up my place for him. I considered the matter for a long time, and this morning I could not go out to work. I wrote him a note and he sent back his reply through Baratz. He suggested that we both go back to work, so the situation is not as desperate as I thought. He will stay on and so will I. I feel lonely here, and it makes me angry.'

'Summer, 1913.

'My dear,

'My life has changed in only one respect—you are not here and I miss you. Nothing else matters. Kinneret no longer calls me and no longer holds any promise for me. I go there in the daytime, but not at night, because without you it has lost its charm. When we used to go swimming there in the mornings, the lake seemed so much more beautiful. Why can't we sit there and gaze at it in silence, as we used to once? The kibbutz members cannot see how you can be a working partner, and I can see a whole world in you.

'What will the end be? I am the only one wielding a hay fork now. My only companion is my revolver. The others are ill. It is hard work and demands a great deal of energy. Life is all work at the moment.

'Degania has come alive now. Families will grow up and live here despite all the difficulties. Today there was a small meeting of seven members. We met to allocate the work, but there were arguments and various people offered to leave if it would make life easier for the others. The result was that the meeting broke up without allocating any jobs, and tomorrow nobody will know what to do. But what do I care if everything turns upside down, as long as I have Devora! If I were to leave Degania would the sun cease to shine? Would my nationalist feelings diminish? Would the soil of Palestine no longer soak up my sweat?

'Before dawn, when the watchman comes to wake me, my lips murmur "Devora", for the sound of your name rings sweetly in my ears. Whatever I am doing and wherever I am, two words are running through my mind the whole time—Devora and Sedjera. Sometimes I feel like shouting at everybody: "None of you knows anything! On the other side of the hills, among those fields, is Sedjera, and at Sedjera . . . ."

'I am counting the days till the weekend. Then I shall walk or ride through Beit Gan, Sarona and Kafr Kanna to Sedjera. I shall pass through the settlement and come to the farm, and perhaps at its entrance I shall meet her whose image constantly fills my thoughts . . .

'It is hard work ploughing the heavy, lumpy soil. My hands ache with the strain, but the pain does not stop me from thinking of you. The surroundings are beautiful. There are so many different colours in the mountains and the fields, the sky and the lake. As I ride home I can see in my imagination Devora waiting joyfully to greet me, but a heavy downpour of rain brings me back to reality.

'Then my thoughts run away with me again. . . . In a few years' time there will be houses at Degania and life will be different. After a day's work, we shall go back to our room with its excellent library. People will come and visit us in order to hear you read aloud from the Russian classics you have translated into Hebrew, and I shall also listen with pleasure.

'Even if it rains on Friday, it will not stop me from coming to Sedjera. Write to me every day. Your letters are all I read. Without you life is empty and boring.'

To a fellow member:

'I told myself that I must be strong, and yet it is just now that I have become weak. Perhaps it is because of my ear operation. Do I miss Degania? When will I return? Every hour I am away costs me blood. There is a buzzing in my ears, and every time the doctor visits the ward, I hope it will get better.

'As for Devora, it is no pleasure to speak about the matter. If an immigrant comes to Palestine looking for moral values, he comes to

Degania to find what he lacks, and Degania asks him to give something in return. Has Degania itself nothing more to give? You have not been able to realise Devora's spiritual strength, which could have enriched Degania so much.'

To Devora again:

'In you I have found all that my soul craves for. An hour ago I rode in from the fields, my heart as cold as the blade of the plough I dragged behind me. Now my heart longs for you. Where are you, my beloved? If you were beside me I would be at ease. As it is, all I can do now is to write to you. Yesterday I helped two newcomers, secondary schoolboys, to settle in—Eliahu Golomb and Dov Hos. Then I read and re-read your letter.

'I could not sleep all night because I had a headache and earache, but let's not talk about that. Yosef asked me how to apportion the expenses of my stay in hospital, and we agreed that I should pay half—100 francs. If you were to come and see me, we could talk and talk about the future.

'Today I put on the shirt you made me, and everyone asked me where I got it from. I just smiled. Dear Devora! In all that I say and all that I think, you are in my mind and in my heart. My head is aching and there is a buzzing in my ears, but I shall try and fall asleep and dream of you.'

'My dear,

'My heart is so full that I do not even want to pick up my pen, because it cannot help me much in any case. I know that life is cruel and that no one can put my difficulties to rights. It is then that I turn to you, because you are so wise, and everything seems good and easy. Then the thought intrudes once again: "Why is good repaid with evil? Why do idealists have to wander far and wide in search of bread?" '

'My beloved, you have taught me to stand firm and be without fear, and I thank you for it. Some months ago I was consumed with doubts, but I overcame them, because with you I feel firm ground under my feet, and my life is complete. I am a worker on the land. Every day my links with the soil, with my comrades, and with a communal way of life free from pettiness, grow stronger. For we are all possessed by an ideal—a completely Jewish life without blemish.

53

'My life is full of joy, for I am in my country, my motherland. I love my language, and every day it grows richer and more full of life. Work, my country and my language—to them I dedicate my youth and my strength. Here I am learning and educating myself in the company of my comrades, reading our literature and absorbing its spirit. I am putting down roots in my motherland, and that is good. In my hours of rest I lie on my back on the ground and raise my voice in song because my doubts have vanished. I can see in my imagination how we shall build the foundation of a national life. Stone by stone we are rebuilding the land laid waste thousands of years ago. I am dedicated to my work and happy that I am one of the builders.'

'I came to Degania in the evening and everyone was sitting on the balcony. Nobody welcomed me warmly, and no fond kisses were forthcoming, but their love was obvious, and now I believe in love and am content. Why am I looking out of the window? Beracha, Liova and Rivka are on their way to the kitchen, but where is Devora? My eyes grow dim with regret, my heart contracts, and I walk away from the window. I reach the dining hall exactly on time, though I know that I shall not find you there. They asked me why I did not invite you to the celebrations and why you did not come. I told them that you do not want to come to Degania just now. Degania, as usual, needs girls. Life here has improved, and despite the fact that there are not many people, the work is well organised. Next year we shall have twenty people because there is so much to do.

'The accounts have been completed and there is a profit of 4,780 francs. Every member gets 100 francs. My infected ear is no better.'

'I return from work and come home, but I do not know what for. The minutes before the bell rings for the evening meal are long and boring. I am writing to you at night, sitting at a table in the kitchen. If anything at Degania has changed at all it is the lamps—they no longer stand on the tables, but are suspended from the ceiling. I dare not think of going to Metulla for a rest. At this moment I cannot even consider going away from Degania. As for you, I would advise you not to return here for at least a month, even though it is a hard life here for me without you. Please do not neglect to take quinine every day, because cases of malaria are on the increase, especially among people who have gone from one place to another. If you do not take quinine regularly, you will not get any benefit from your stay at a summer resort.

'Your letters, my love, bring me happiness and joy. Do not worry about me, for I am not dangerously ill and manage most of the time to divert my mind from my pain. Your letters are like springs of pure, clear water, and every word, every idea, is refreshing and warming. As far as the types of children you want to write about are concerned, I am sure that you will be able to set down in writing the emotions they arouse in you when you see them. I am looking forward with pleasure to the appearance of your book, and it seems to me that your inspiration is deepening and broadening, and I am proud because of it.

'The days go on and on and it seems like years since we last saw each other. I cannot imagine that you will stay in Judaea for two years to learn the language, so far from me. And what about money? You ought to start thinking about Kinneret. I bought some citrons and sent them to your parents.

'Today I shall be at Ein Ganim and tomorrow in Jaffa at the doctor's, so I shall finish this letter then. I walk about the streets and wish that I could meet you, wanting you to be in places where I know it is impossible for you to be. I read and make conversation, meet people, see new places, and it is all worthless, because you are not there. I am happy in the knowledge that you live within me.

'My dear, it had seemed to me that my family feeling had weakened with time and withered away. My parents' tears did not move me, and I left them. It was cruel of me to abandon my parents to their loneliness. But you have reawakened that feeling within me. My heart is stirring and I feel longing and pity for them, because they are old now.'

And again, this time from Jaffa:

'This is a bright place, and the fragrance of citrus groves is part of its character. All my feelings are burgeoning within me—life is beautiful! In the evenings the carriages drive to and fro, their occupants enjoying the fresh, revivifying air of spring. I stand on the verandah of the Spector Hotel and am full of longing. Where is my darling? For a moment it seemed as if you were beside me.

E

55

You are a part of everything I do. I do not belong to myself any more. You and I—both of us—share one body and one soul.

'There is no interest for me in the library, or in the club, or even in people. They are all good . . . but someone is missing. As soon as I arrived I went to see Dr. Sherman and he gave me some drops which have eased the pain. Nobody writes from Degania. My relations in Ein Ganim send you their regards.'

'I am attending the doctor and my ear is healing up. Yosef Bussel came and stayed here for a day. After New Year he is going to visit Hulda and Kfar Uriah. I hope that I shall be better by then and be able to come home. He arranged with Ruppin that we should get a grant for a threshing machine and a water pump. Saplings have been planted and lucerne sown. This needed strength and energy, and you know how things are with us just now.

'I had an intimate talk with Bussel. He informed me that we have not been included in the various decisions that have been made. He hopes that people will mend their ways, and that everything will work out all right. Just the same, I cannot agree to the rule of one individual, or even a few individuals.

'It looks as if the teachers' training courses are being wound up, so you need not regret not having enrolled for them.'

'I am writing from Hadera and I feel strange and not at all well. My eyes are half closed and my dreams are full of dread. The trees in the forest are swaying as though rocking to rest my imagination, my will and my ideals. You could rest here from Degania's burning sun. You would feel better here, and being yourself again you would dance, bringing even the shadows to life, even though your talents have weakened a little of late.

'Some weeks ago I complained that you do not feel what I tell you with so much emotion. And I remember the time, four years ago, when I came to Hadera. It was a clear night, and the forest told me: "These are not trees. Can't you see, they are the souls of the heroes who gave their lives in draining these swamps here!" In my imagination I saw young men with turiyahs on their shoulders and eucalyptus seedlings in their hands, hurrying to the swamps. Each one planted a tree and was swallowed up by the mud and water, and a tree grew in the swamp over every one of the bodies buried there. In my dream I was a labourer at Hadera and suffered from loneliness. I left there ashamed and with my soul cast down, for those who came before me had left their souls at Hadera and had not flinched from danger. Yet I, whose duty it was to carry on, did not do so, to my shame. The trees sway and the shadows lengthen. Darkness and loneliness conquer all in this place.'

'I could not write earlier for pain, much as I wanted to, and much as I wanted to talk to you. My hand wrote and told you not to come, but my heart believed you would. I cannot ask you to leave your place at Degania, for the work there is pressing. And not only work! Please do not keep yourself at a distance. Come to me, and understanding too will come in the course of time. Now I believe that you will stay on at Degania. In my heart I am praying that you will succeed, that you will win through.

'I was very happy to receive your letter—the few words you wrote, rather—from Tiberias. They transported me to a world where everything was good. While Yisrullik and Yitzhak were speaking to me in Haifa hospital, I lay there with my eyes wide open but did not see them. The sun was sinking in an aura of green. The sea, the mighty, calm, beautiful sea, brought me peace and rest. The hospital resounded with groaning and weeping, and through the wall I could hear a child on the other side crying bitterly. Nevertheless, it seemed as if I were not a part of that world, and I even ignored my own pain.

'Somebody came and gave me your letter. It brought me new strength and my weakness retreated. "I shall not forget you when I look at the lake", you wrote. Can you even think of forgetting me? I can forget myself but never you. How could I, when you are implanted in me?

'I have decided to take a trip to Beirut and should like you to come with me. I hope you will come, and then we can go by ship from Haifa, leaving on Friday and arriving in Beirut on Saturday.

'When I came to the hotel this morning, I found many new arrivals from Russia, including Ossia Trumpeldor and other acquaintances. They were glad to see me and I accompanied them to the ship. They were travelling by sea from Beirut to Jaffa, via Haifa. I wrote to you from Haifa and then spent a night on deck. It was wonderful. A pair of lovers sat opposite me, but I did not envy them, because now I am no longer poorer than they.

'I remembered Hamsun who tells how he gave the sparkle from his eyes to his beloved. Is this essential? Will there be days when my eyes will not sparkle? And will you remember that conversation when we told each other that we had never loved and would never love anyone else and that this was our only love forever? I agree, without love there is no life. Our lives are lives of love and longing, and with your talent you could portray them in a book. Write, and so improve your story-telling! You must write, both for your own enjoyment and the enjoyment of others. Materially, we are not badly off. My hero Hamsun was not affected by material considerations.

'I went to see the Professor and he has begun treatment. In two days' time they will operate. My darling, my only one. I turn to you and tell you all, for to whom else should I turn? I have not confided in my parents for years, because we have grown very much apart. When I was a child, my mother travelled to the county town to take me to the dentist and her caresses eased my pain. Now she knows nothing about me, my happiness or my illness. The mighty ocean lies between us, and so does the ocean of life. Sometimes I have the impression that you consider my attitude to my parents to be weak. Well, it is and it isn't. There are moments when . . . . My darling, when you are mine I shall be worthy and good.

Kisses,

Shmuel'.

'I have sinned against you. For some days now my ear has not pained me. I have been walking idly about the town and have not written. There is no explanation for this at all.

'I am in Beirut. I live in a hotel, undergo medical examinations, look at the life of the port. There are many law students here. Everybody except me seems to be studying something. When the pain gets better and I wander about with nothing to do, I do not like it. I glanced in a mirror and saw how bad I look. Will you be able to settle down at Sedjera? And the language, does it find a place in your heart? Do you feel that it will serve as a bridge between you and the land and its people? And between you and me also? Or are you only learning the language because, as an intelligent person, you cannot bear not to understand the language of the country you live in? Sometimes I think that you would not be learning it, were it not for your contact with me. If this is true, and your love for me is the reason, good! I would dearly like you to

58

learn the language so that you may understand the land and its people'.

'Beirut—I wish I could be free of this ear infection. I want to be happy, but cannot. Still, Beirut is beautiful.

'After you left, I suffered terribly. Nobody who has not had this illness can imagine how much. Today, when I arrived, my temperature had risen. Webster, the famous specialist, will be here in three months' time, but meanwhile there are only ordinary doctors here. Despite the pain, I go for walks in the beautiful surroundings. The sea view is enchanting. How am I? I am fine because I am in love. The world is ours. I feel ready for an operation, but have my doubts about being operated on by a non-Jew. What am I to him, and who is he? I withdrew 100 francs from the office and came to Beirut. You are short of money I know. Take some in Tiberias, do not be shy. Take the material you need. It is the custom to give a new person credit, and perhaps you will work a little at Sedjera. Tomorrow I shall go and see a French professor at the University here.'

'Beirut—I am writing this in bed. Just this minute I sent you a telegram saying that in a day or two I shall be up and about again. Today things are not too good, but they will improve tomorrow. It is much better after the operation than before it, but I am not entirely unconcerned. I have nosebleed all the time and they cannot stop it. Nevertheless, the professors say that I will be discharged from hospital in a couple of days. I should like to feel an improvement in my condition before I leave, and be able to go on my way without this pain in my ear and my head. My patience will run out though, and I shall leave as soon as possible.

'They operated today, Saturday morning, without anaesthetic. The pain was so bad . . . During the night I felt better, so I got up and went out. The whole world seemed to be enveloped in mist. The air was wintry, and I wanted to sit in a sledge, with flowers in my hand, and ride around a little. The things one thinks of! I may come back via Damascus. Where will you be, and how are you? I know you worry about me, but do not. Be happy, my beloved!'

This is how I became ill. We used to sleep by the heaps of cleaned seeds in the storehouse, our rifles close to hand. The watchmen used to patrol outside, guarding the fruits of our year's toil. Suddenly I was awakened by a mosquito stinging me and buzzing in my ear. I stood up agitatedly, not understanding what had happened.

I told the watchman and he said he would look after me. It was three o'clock in the morning, and I sat in the kitchen while he warmed some olive oil, and then poured it into my right ear. 'This will kill the mosquito', he said. Apparently he overheated the olive oil. . . .

What happened to the mosquito I do not know, but from then on there was a continuous stinging sensation in my ear, as if something were piercing it deep inside. There was only one otologist in Palestine, in Jaffa. The journey to Jaffa took several days. The doctor examined my ear with an otoscope, put some drops in, and sent me home. But the pain did not abate, and after months of going to the Jaffa doctor without any result, I travelled to Beirut. There a professor from the American college operated on my nose and I returned home the next day.

When I left the train at Zemach I met some of the members, carrying heavy sacks on their backs, and I volunteered to give them a helping hand. As I lifted one of the sacks, the wound inside my nose opened and blood streamed from it. There was no doctor at Degania or Kinneret, and the chemist had nothing to staunch the flow of blood. However we learnt that the chemist at Milhamia (Menachemia) did have the remedy we needed. This was on a Saturday and darkness was already falling. A young settler, Moshe Barsky, who had not been long in Palestine and had only recently joined the kibbutz, volunteered to ride to Milhamia and ask the chemist there for the medicament we needed to stop the flow of blood. Soon after he had set out, a gang of Arabs ambushed him near Kfar Ovadiah and murdered him. The next day, in broad daylight, the same gang killed another Jewish boy while he was ploughing at Kinneret, and stole his mules. A few days later these same Arabs killed a watchman at Sedjera.

The settlers of Galilee were very angry and immediately began a search for the murderers. Meanwhile, Tanchum rode off to try and find the stolen mules.

Despite all that the Middle Eastern doctors could do, the pain in my ear grew worse. After a whole year of ineffective treatments, the kibbutz treasurer's department held long discussions about the big expense of sending me to Europe for treatment, but could come to no positive decision. I decided that I would go to Vienna independently. It so happened that just at that time an epidemic broke out among our cattle. Yosef Bussel, the kibbutz organiser, asked me to go to the Palestine Office in Jaffa, on my way to catch my ship to Europe, and ask for assistance.

'Dear Dayan', Bussel wrote, 'when you get to Jaffa you must speak to the Office about building a proper cowshed. Make it clear to them that it is because of the shed we are using at present that our cattle have been attacked by disease. They must either send people at once to put up a proper building or give us the money for it, and we will try to build it ourselves. Several cows are ill and a calf has died. All my good wishes for your journey, and may you return soon, fit and well.'

Yosef Bussel had no idea what the disease was that was attacking our cattle, but he was sure of the necessity for a stone-built cowshed. That is why he had asked me to explain to 'them' at the Palestine Office that building should not be delayed.

'Haifa—My mood has changed. I am pleased at the prospect of a sea journey and trips to the mountains, although it is very trying to have to wait in Haifa for two days for the sea to calm down. The ships' agents will let us know whether or not we can anchor at Jaffa. I am going to the ship, though I do not know whether we shall sail.

'Please tell Yosef Bussel that I spoke to Dunia and he will either visit Degania or write. Dostrovsky has just told me that there is no coal.'

'Haifa—I am on my way from Haifa to Jaffa. Even though it is stormy, I hope to be able to go ashore there. Perhaps I'll go ashore at Port Said as well. Be cheerful and then I will be also. Do not worry, and be careful of the damp. Write to me, so that I can forget my troubles.'

'Trieste—Yesterday evening I left the ship. Since I set out I have crossed Egypt by rail and made a sea journey to Italy. I landed at Brindisi and took the train from there. It passed through beautiful country which captivates the eye. I am a Jewish youth, athirst for everything, though not everything quenches my thirst. Trieste is an Italian city which belongs to Austria, and its inhabitants have angry faces. I shall leave by the slow train—22 hours to Vienna—and finish this letter there.

'The journey has been interesting, but I have been troubled by the situation you find yourself in. It is unhealthy and very difficult to undertake a journey to Russia in the winter, especially if one's means are slender.

'Will your letters reach Vienna? I wrote to Degania in the language I love. Please forgive me, although you could not read them. I could not bring myself to write to you in Yiddish'.

I arrived in Vienna and walked until I reached the Jewish ghetto. There the same feeling came over me again that I had managed to lose in my six years in Palestine. I met Diaspora Jews again. I met Jewish migrants in their hostels and ran from them, because I could not breathe in that atmosphere. At the same time, I was filled with sympathy and pity for Jews who cannot see that our country awaits them.

When I put my hand to the plough I forgot my people and its suffering, a people reviled and scorned, yet a people which does not try and save itself.

In boots and a short coat, the work of a Tiberias tailor, I sailed from Jaffa and arrived in Vienna. In my bag I had five gold Napoleons (a loan from my brother), and I had packed my clothes in a padlocked wooden box. The clothes I was wearing, and the fact that I was carrying my wooden box attracted the glances of passers-by. From the station I went on foot to a modest hotel in a street in the Jewish quarter.

Next day I went to Dr. Falk, head of the Zionist Federation in Vienna, and presented my letter of introduction from Dr. Tahon. Dr. Falk could not understand my Yiddish, but Tahon's letter explained everything. After greeting me and reading the letter, he picked up the telephone and rang a doctor friend of his at one of the hospitals, who agreed to see me. Dr. Falk then called his daughter, who could hardly refrain from laughing at my strange dress and the way I spoke, and she took me to the hospital by tram.

It was a small, private Christian hospital, and I was received there with sympathy and politeness. I was asked about the treatment I had had earlier in Jaffa and Beirut, and about the unnecessary operation on my nose. The doctors gathered round me and listened, read the medical certificates and burst out laughing. The next day I had an operation on my ear. It took ten days to heal, and while I was in hospital I was visited regularly by Dr. Falk, his wife, his daughter and his friends.

In January (1914), Dr. Falk sent me a letter which said:
'My dear Mr. Dayan,

Since you no longer need to stay in hospital, I have arranged with the doctor in charge that you should leave on Monday. Please come and see me and I will advise you what to do further. Today I wrote to the Palestine Office and told them that you will be able to leave Vienna in about ten days'.

In the meantime I wrote to Devora, then on the eve of her journey to Russia.

'Vienna—Devora, the doctor has promised that he will operate on my ear tomorrow, Saturday morning. I had no difficulty in getting into hospital.

'Outside it is miserable. The sky is overcast, and snow is falling. I have not seen the sun for a week. Since we took leave of each other life has come to a standstill. Here I am in the centre of Europe, full of excitement at what I shall see and the pleasure I shall have. And how do I spend my time? In hospital, waiting for an operation.'

'Vienna—In two hours' time I go into hospital, and when I leave it I hope to be well. They will operate within the next few days. The doctor says there is nothing to worry about, I shall be all right by the time I leave. The nose operation I had in Beirut was unnecessary and harmful.'

'Vienna—Shalom, shalom my dearly beloved. I can already sit up and even walk a few steps. This is progress indeed, four days after a serious operation! They operated on Saturday morning and I awoke at noon, after it was all over. The pain has lessened now, but I felt very weak when I got out of bed. The doctor has promised that I shall make a full recovery, and shall be leaving hospital in a few days.

'When we meet I shall be well, though I have become thinner. Perhaps I shall be able to eke out my money and come to Russia, returning to Palestine from there. So far not a word from you. Perhaps the postman will bring a greeting tomorrow.

'You have started to work, and the tempo is rising, I read several times in your letter—I have waited with mounting excitement for your next letter. Till it comes I shall re-read this one. You should by now have received the money and clothes I sent to Jaffa.

'According to my reckoning you will reach Cherkass on January 15th. Begin treatment immediately because you have to be a farmer's wife. We shall return together to work on the land. Our plans for a world tour are likely to be an obstacle to our working on the land, for the city is attractive and life is easy there. That is how things are with every nation and that is how they are with us. But we shall not abandon the land, for without work on the land there is no pleasure in our lives. For that reason we must beware of jobs which might draw us away from country life. We can discuss these matters in detail when we meet.

'Of course, you feel the same way as I do about these matters. I received *Hapoel Hatzair* and *Hashiloah* and enjoyed reading them. In two weeks' time my ear will be better. I still do not know whether I shall go to Russia, even for a short stay, and risk imprisonment there. Still, I have not forgotten the plans we made at Degania. I shall wait and see what you think, and look forward with eagerness to your next letter'.

'Devora! My dressing has just been renewed, and now I have taken *Homo Sapiens* from under my pillow and have begun reading it. It is giving me a great deal of pleasure and I thank you for it. I was so impatient for the mail to come with a letter from you, after eight days in Vienna. Instead I received, not a letter, but a telegram saying, 'How did the operation go?' Before I opened the envelope I thought it was from you. In Beirut, when I had my first operation, nobody wrote to me and I was very lonely. You were the first to write then, and afterwards you came to see me. This time the telegram was from my parents, and a wave of warm feeling swept over me, as if my mother had kissed me.

'As for me, if I go straight back to Palestine I shall not forgive myself for missing an opportunity that will never recur. To be in Europe and not to see something of it would be so wrong. Here I am in the cultural centre of the world. It is so fascinating, how can I close my eyes to it!

'A woman has been visiting the patient next to me all morning. She keeps kissing him on the forehead, and then they talk together in low tones. I envy them. If you were beside me we should have a great deal to talk about. Devora, I have already told you that I must get away for a time from the place I have lived in and from the people I have been so closely involved with for a number of years. I have not known any other way of life during those years, and I want to get away on my own for a while. After all, I haven't seen the world yet. I would be so happy, if I could live a spiritual life for at least a year and then return. It would have a great influence on my future life. When I left my father's house and my home town I was a youngster, and it is most unlikely that I shall ever be able to leave Palestine again. When we return to Palestine I do not know how we shall start our life together.

'My darling, there was no post today either. I am worried and restless. Has something happened to you? I want to send a telegram but do not know where you are. I would have sent a telegram to Cherkass but do not want to start your parents worrying. Please write now. I am sending your mother a letter, but I shall not mention the state of your health. Keep well and be happy. Lots of kisses.'

Yeruham Klebanov wrote:

'My dear Dayan,

I sat down to write to you, but do not know whether I shall be able to, because there is nothing to say about the work here. Tanchum will certainly have told you all about it. A few days ago we finished the sowing and afterwards returned from the fields together. Suddenly everyone decided to celebrate, and people started singing and firing their rifles and revolvers. You can imagine how angry I was. 'What is this', I thought to myself, 'how can anyone at Degania be in festive mood now? Have they already forgotten Moshe Barsky, or are they trying to show how brave and courageous they are?' One of our members had been killed, and here the rest of them were, going gay, as if nothing had happened. Could they have been so cheerful if they had lost a brother or a parent only two months previously? If Moshe were to rise from the grave and return to the place for which he had laid down his life, he would see that nothing had changed. Then he might well think that he had died for nothing . . . Ah, well, I had better not say any more.

'Congratulations on your recovery. Now that you are over your illness, we all hope that you will be strong and well and return to your work, as in years gone by. You must come back to Degania as soon as possible, not alone, but with her—and then perhaps we'll dance!

'We have so far received only one letter from Devora, while she was on the way to Russia. I had already written to her and am still waiting for an answer. Will you go to Russia or come straight back to Palestine? I do not think you will go to Russia.

'Write and let us know how you are, when you are coming out of hospital, and what you intend to do then. Forgive me for writing so little, but you know how difficult it is to write at all, especially the first few evenings after the sowing is finished.   Yeruham.'

And again, from my letter to Devora from Vienna:

'I have not seen you for twenty days, or heard you speak or laugh, or call my name. Why haven't you written to me yet? I have just put down *Homo Sapiens*. I am enjoying the book, but am very anxious about your health. I got up and walked about, and I feel that I am getting my strength back. Isn't that enough, to be well! But my Devora is much more ill than I am, and why don't I make her better? Yesterday the good Dr. Falk came to visit me. He brought me some chocolate and we talked for a long time.

'I dreamt that you came to Vienna and paid me a surprise visit in hospital. I am fed up with being ill, or as you put it, with "our ear". The doctor says that I shall have to stay in hospital for another two weeks, even though I have already been here for eleven days. Next to me there is another patient who is having trouble with his ears. He is a dark fellow of about 30. His mother is visiting him at the moment. Every so often she turns away from him and sheds a tear, while his wife strokes his head.

'Devora! I sit here like a man in a dream and think about the happiness you have given me. You left Europe and its treasures behind you and went to an unknown land. There you became as if born again, and have established a new life for yourself.'

Brief mention has already been made of Moshe Barsky, whose grave was the first one at Degania. He was murdered on November 22nd 1913, on the way from Milhamia to Degania. Six Arabs wanted to steal the mule he was riding, so they shot him in the back. The mule galloped off to Degania and Moshe fought back gallantly.

His attackers made off, leaving behind a shoe, a club and a large wicker basket. Nobody knows how long it took Moshe to die, but when we found him he was already dead. He was the newest, youngest member of our group, and had volunteered to ride to Milhamia to see if he could get something from the chemist there to stop my nosebleed. When his mule arrived in the yard riderless, we went out with lanterns to look for him. We found his body in a field near the river.

Moshe was a country boy from a village near Kiev. He knew the ways of the peasants, and was well versed in river lore, fishing, farming and horses. His love of nature and his Zionist upbringing had brought him to Palestine. Nature and his work filled his life, and he had been at Degania since the first day he set foot in the country.

He was very young, not yet nineteen, but in the eight months he lived with us he forged strong links with all of us, with the place itself and with our work. Only death could have broken them. He had not ever seen anything of the country except for the settlements of Lower Galilee. He had been looking forward to exploring Upper Galilee the following Passover . . .

We buried him in the olive grove where he had worked, and raised a small mound over his grave. The next day we harnessed several pairs of mules, and some of the younger members of the kibbutz started ploughing the field where Moshe had been killed. The ploughmen slung their rifles from the mules' reins and wore cartridge belts across their shoulders. They were ready for anything, and as they followed their ploughs they were burning with anger and the desire for revenge. We had arranged that in the event of an attack we would unharness the mules and let them make their own way back to Degania, while we would fight back. But there were no attacks, and our desire for revenge gradually faded and was replaced by bitter grief at Moshe's death.

I wrote to his family in Russia on behalf of the kibbutz.

'Twenty of us, young men and girls, left our parents' homes and returned to the land of our fathers with the desire to build, to create, and to make a future for ourselves here. Among us lived and worked Moshe, of blessed memory, your son and our brother. He lived among us for only a short time, eight months, but this was still long enough for him to have forged links with us which we shall never forget.

'Your dear son was dear to us also, and his memory will be dear to the nation he came to Palestine to help to create. He gave his young strength to the cause, and his blood to the soil of our land, the land of our fathers, the land we are fighting for now. We can feel your grief, for it is also ours, and Moshe is deeply graven in our hearts.

'Our consolation lies in the knowledge that your son Moshe's death has deepened and increased in our souls the certainty that we must fight with all our strength and not retreat. We must achieve victory and clothe our vision in reality, the vision of our forebears, the people of Israel.

'Yours in the building of Zion, and with all our sympathy, kibbutz Degania'.

The Barsky family sent the following reply:

'Great as our sorrow is, we shall not weep or lament. Dear sons, work with energy and hope that our people may be strengthened! We are sending you our second son, Shalom, the brother of Moshe. He will take Moshe's place within your ranks. Moshe's death will bring us all to Palestine. We are coming! . . . . .

And they did. First Shalom came, then the eldest of the family, Harma, then their mother and other brothers, and finally their father. They settled in Kfar Yehezkiel, Kfar Vitkin and Yokneam. When Degania's second boy was born to Devora and myself, we called him Moshe.

After the murder, the police came. Instead of concentrating on finding the murderers, however, they busied themselves with the sick man, myself, on whose behalf the murdered man had set out on his journey. They looked on me as the cause of Moshe's death. They based their investigation on the theory that I had been in love with the murdered man's sister. The Government investigator, the genius who dreamed up this theory, was a Jew from Tiberias.

The same week we received a telegram from the Palestine Office. 'Have just heard awful news of murder. Have no words to express our grief. Have telegraphed to Mr. Hankin to visit you at once'.

On Monday evening, the day after Barsky's burial, three members of Kinneret were returning from their fields after a day's ploughing. They were attacked by four Arabs with rifles and Yosef Saltzmann was badly wounded. He died some hours later.

The news of the attack caused great anger and excitement, not only at Kinneret, but in the entire neighbourhood, for Barsky's murder was still fresh in our memories. We immediately sent out search parties on horseback and on foot to find the murderers. Once again, however, they had disappeared in the wadi, and when darkness fell the search was abandoned.

The authorities tried to find the murderers in the Beisan and Jezreel Valley areas, but they had crossed the Jordan from the east, and had made good their escape. Yosef Saltzmann was buried at the spot where he was murdered, on the road from Tiberias to Milhamia. The members of Kinneret passed there every day on the way to their fields.

Then Ya'acov Feldman, the watchman at Sedjera, was murdered. At four o'clock in the morning, shortly before his guard duty was due to finish, Feldman heard suspicious noises. He was patrolling the boundary of Sedjera, which was marked by a stone wall, and the noises came from the other side of it. The night was dark and rainy and it was difficult to see anything, but straining his eyes in the darkness, Feldman saw the blurred shapes of several people trying to get into the yard. At the same moment they saw him too, and before he could raise his rifle they shot him through the head. His fellow watchman rushed over to Yavniel and broke the news. The watchman there had a tracker dog, brought over from abroad, but before the dog could even get a sniff at the scent the rain had washed it out, so Feldman's assailants were never found.

The murders strengthened our resolution and that of the other Galilee settlements to take every measure possible to protect our lives and property.

When Devora was ill, I wrote to her:

'I am in Tiberias and am very sorry that your treatment is so difficult to bear. Soon I hope to find you well and gay, and no longer in pain. I shall come when threshing is finished. Get well soon.

'At the moment I am working in the citrus grove, and as I move among the trees I think of you and of the farm. I am glad you have left here because life is very difficult in this terrific heat. I have got a visitor. My sister Bathsheba has come to work in Galilee and has been staying in our room for the past week. The work is going forward all right, and the barley has already been threshed. There are only two mounds of wheat to thresh, and then we shall go over to Kinneret. The harvest this year is better than we had calculated, and we shall probably make a profit on the wheat and the barley. The citrus grove looks quite different now that the locusts have departed, and everything is fresh and green. Yeruham has returned from his work in the city and brought toys for our child.

Yours with kisses,
Shmuel'.

'Love of my life,

'I am writing to you because I am very unhappy. Yesterday Bathsheba tried to drown herself in the Jordan, but the water delivered her up. She was brought safely ashore and back here. Please do not grieve about this. Get well darling, because our happiness depends on it.' But Tanchum and I had words over the sorry affair. I wrote him:

'What you said about my trip to Jerusalem has wounded me very deeply. It is hurtful to realise that you have not tried to understand the crux of the matter, how much a person can suffer. It has never happened that I, who am always careful to avoid unnecessary expenditure, should overstep the mark where medical help is concerned. Someone who is seriously ill must have adequate treatment. In a place like Degania, where the climate and conditions are inclined to make people ill in any case, adequate medical help is essential. Otherwise it would be impossible to live here.

'It is well known that my sister did not spare herself at work. Nobody will gainsay this fact and it is quite possibly the reason for her illness. Dr. Sherman says she has anaemia. Is she supposed to neglect this and not receive treatment?

' "You have forgotten that she is a working girl," you said to me. Does a working girl have to remain in the state she is in? This time I must go with her and find out exactly what is wrong and how to cure it, even if she is a working girl and has no money. It was very insulting of you to call this extravagance.

Shmuel'.

Tanchum replied:

'I am deeply sorry that I hurt you like that. If I had realised how

I. Working in the orange groves near Petach
Tikva in 1910.

II. One of the first mud huts in Um-Juni—which later became Degania, the first commune.

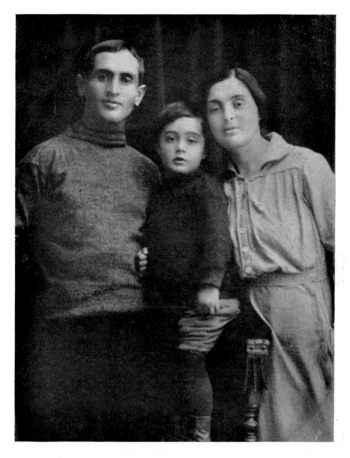

III. With my wife Devora, and our first-born, Moshe, at Degania, 1918.

IV. Back on a visit
to Russia in 1919.

V. My wife in 1910.

VI. Nahalal—the co-operative settlement in its first years.

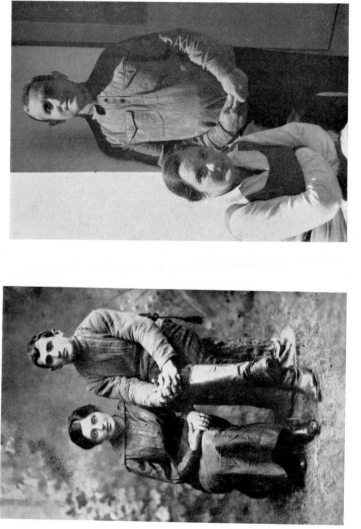

VIII. And at Nahalal in 1937.

VII. With Devora at Kiev in 1914.

IX. Near the cow shed on our farm at Nahalal, 1947.

X. Zohar, our youngest
son, in 1947. The last
picture taken before
he was killed in the
Israeli-Arab war.

XI. Aviva, our daughter,
in A.T.S. uniform,
Cairo, 1945.

you would feel, 1 would never have said what I did, believe me. You know I make no exceptions as far as medical treatment is concerned, and my opinion would be no different if it were I who were ill. However, I want to calm your mood now. While you are on your journey, please do not think about what has happened. Go in peace, and get well, both of you. Perhaps I was wrong about Bathsheba this time. I wish to make today my day of atonement and ask both your pardons. Go in peace.'

Again to Devora:

'My dear, I found our son, Musinka, well. He likes the other children and is satisfied with the life there. He is coughing much less, and immediately asked how you were. I told you you were getting better and gave him some sweets, which he shared with the other children. After he had been given his quinine he lay down muttering "chocolate, sweets", and just before he dropped off to sleep he asked me if you have a comfortable bed. My dear, the sun shone so beautifully today and the view is so wonderful. Why are we so disconsolate? Even now, in the evening I am sitting in our room and feeling sad and forlorn.'

'Why should I try and hide the fact that, however much effort I make, I cannot look after Moshe the way you do? He misses you a lot. Rainy days are the worst of all. I can understand how you feel in Jerusalem and your attitude to people and affairs. How can I set your mind at rest? Do not cry, darling. What if we do miss you? It is good to miss someone. I can supply the boy's needs, entertain him, and hold his hand. Sometimes I scold him. In the evenings I wash him and slip into bed beside him. He snuggles up to me and embraces me, putting his little arms round my neck. My heart melts, and tears roll on to our dear little child's face and eyes. I kiss him and fall asleep. I wake up in the middle of the night, undress in the dark, and get back into bed, feeling very tired. I get up early. I am reading Dostoievsky now and everything he writes about the soul of man stifles all desire to sleep. Tanchum and Baratz have gone to Damascus by wagon to earn some money.

With kisses, Shmuel'.

'Your letter saddened me, because of the eye infection you and Moshe are suffering from. It is difficult for me to picture how you look now. Here Baratz has been lying on his back with his eyes closed, while you are in a bad way and even worse off for medical aid than we are. I am very worried about the child's eyes. I understood just how bad things are from your letter and I hope they will improve.

'This time I cannot send you any provisions because there is nobody to send them with. I shall send you everything at the first opportunity. There have been many changes at Degania. Yeruham, Dov and Yehoshua have left for good. The general meetings go on as before. We have not yet finished storing all the grain and are working desperately hard night and day with insufficient numbers. It will take another two or three weeks yet, and even then only some of us will be able to get away.

'At the last meeting we decided to raise our wages to 60 francs and limit credit. Even so, I must try and go away somewhere for a rest, because in my present weak state I shall not be fit to start work in the New Year. On the other hand, I know that even if I do go away I shan't rest, but still. As far as you are concerned, it would be better if you stayed where you are till the New Year. You will get better then, and if it should be necessary to go to Jerusalem, do so. When you are better and the boy has grown a little, we shall be able to make better arrangements.

Kisses, Shmuel'.

CHAPTER THREE

FROM KIBBUTZ TO CO-OPERATIVE VILLAGE

The commune ceased being an experiment, and proved to be a very possible enriching way of life—but would it be a way of life for the thousands of immigrants? For the not-so-idealistic middle aged person, for families? Would everyone be able to yield to the demands a commune makes on the individual?

There were two needs to be met—the need to obtain new land and cultivate new areas, and the need for a second form of agricultural community which would suit those who were unable to live in a commune.

The two were met by setting the example of Nahalal, the co-operative village in the valley of Jezreel—between Haifa and Nazareth.

The ideals of work, mutual help and good social life were kept, but the concept was different. Each farmer would have his piece of land, and would invest in it his work—not to give what he could and receive what he needed, but to give what he wanted to give and receive in accordance with that.

The family would live together, the children would be at home, the social institutes, school, store and so forth would belong to the village as a whole—each farmer paying taxes.

Nahalal was a new solution. There was room for privacy, individualism, initiative—more so than in the commune, and yet it was a small group of people depending on one another and in need of each other's help.

73

The two farms, Degania and Nahalal, offered a way of life to the different types, age groups and characters arriving in Israel. Nahalal, when it was founded, was marshland with malaria, poverty and many moments of despair. Today it is a flourishing village, one of the strongest moshavim with wealthy farms, among which is that of Shmuel Dayan. His children are moshav members, continuing the tradition.

For hundreds of years the Arab village of Mehalol had nestled among the mountain ridges of Nazareth. It was not easy to get to, for there was no proper road. By the time you had clambered over rocks, jumped across gulleys, and stumbled across stretches of uneven ground to the village, three-quarters of a mile from the Government road, you were dripping with sweat.

There was not one tree in the village, nor was there a single flower garden or vegetable plot. The villagers were a wretched lot. The men sat around idly, eastern fashion, telling each other tall stories. Some of the women brought water from a spring some distance away, carrying it in jars on their heads. Other made their daughters work, while they sat and examined their hair and heads for vermin. Children with trachoma-infected eyes and distended bellies rolled about in the dust, while the villagers' scrawny chickens scratched about in the manure heaps for something to eat, all the food they ever got.

There were two mukhtars (village headmen), one Moslem, one Christian, and they hated each other like poison. Two brothers, Turkish officials, owned the village, which they had inherited from their father, and their inheritance had turned them into deadly enemies. There was no doctor in the village, and no medicines.

For the villagers and their families the land was a source of drudgery and suffering. Their farming methods were primitive and monotonous. They just grew maize, durrah (Indian millet) and sesame. They used the ordinary Arab plough to turn over the soil, which gave a very low yield—132 lb. per dunam—and never thought of using manure or fertilisers. Instead of being spread on the worn-out fields, to replace the nourishment taken out of the soil, the manure lay in heaps round the hovels the villagers lived in, filling the whole place with its stench. Weeds flourished in the

74

fields, and as no attempt was made to uproot them, they continually reseeded themselves.

A few scrawny cows grazed among the weeds and swamp plants, champing on them half-heartedly, while they plodded about the fields, as hungry and ill-fed as their owners. The cattle were left out in the fields the whole time, night and day, rain and shine, and during heavy rainstorms they sheltered in caves in the mountains. They gave milk for only three months in the year, and their yield was low—just enough for the needs of their owner. If there should happen to be a slight surplus, the Arab peasant's wife made the two-hour journey over the mountains to Nazareth and back, selling the milk at a very low price, because there were no Europeans to buy it. In fact there was often nobody at all who wanted to buy it.

This was the village, with its thousands of dunams of wasted land, which we decided to turn into an outstanding example of Jewish settlement, once we had bought the land.

The members of the first workers' moshav (co-operative settlement) could not just wait and do nothing until the purchase had been completed. We felt that the hour of achievement was near, and we had to spy out the land of Mehalol, which was to be the site of our settlement.

It was winter, and raining, and a bitter wind was blowing. A broad plain stretched between the mountains with their sleepy villages—the Emek!

Nazareth was at its head, Mount Carmel at its foot. The mountains were craggy and wooded. There were oak, carob and many other kinds of trees. The valley was a closed one, and the horizon was narrow. Wherever one looked there were mountains.

Three of us walked about exploring the valley, and three groups of trees caught our eyes. They looked like groves or orchards. One was not far from the road to the east and we could see some Arab families working among the trees and vegetables. Nearby there was a pond, the water welling up into it from a small spring among the rocks. There was more than enough for all the aubergines, tomatoes, fig trees and lemon trees.

A wadi wound its way through the hills, and several springs emptied into it. Sheep and goats grazed nearby, coming over to wooden troughs now and again to quench their thirst.

We covered the length and breadth of the plain, climbing hills and descending into valleys. We examined the soil, the stubble, the roots, estimated how high the crops had grown, the state of the soil, the size of the yield.

We saw from the first that the land was good. We examined the place and the people who lived there. We had a look at the swamps and found out their extent. Our hearts were filled with mingled hope and fear. We were frightened of malaria, blackwater fever, of unknown difficulties ahead.

We left in silence, our spirits cast down. Then we started to talk about draining the swamps, and whispered words of consolation to ourselves. 'The whole country is full of swamps, so why should we not have our share? We do not want to be pampered.'

Then we met an old man and asked him:

'Grandfather, what are these ruins?'

'A ruined settlement.'

'What sort of settlement?'

'German.'

'What happened?'

'They died.'

'Do you remember the settlement?'

'It all happened when I was a child.'

'Has nobody lived here since then?'

'There was a village here after that, an Arab village.'

'What has happened to it?'

'It has fallen into ruins as well.'

'And the people?'

'They all died', he answered, and turned to go. We stopped him to ask one last question.

'What makes it impossible to live in this spot?'

'Bad wind and bad water. If anyone drinks this water, his belly swells up, and in three days he is dead.'

'He is dead.' 'They died.' 'Two villages destroyed.' These were the thoughts running through our heads. And the third settlement in this place, what reason was there to suppose that it would fare any better than the first two?

We climbed to the top of a high hill, one of the foothills of the thickly wooded mountains of Nazareth. We wanted to look down on the Emek, the valley where we were going to settle. As we climbed the hill we noticed old stones underfoot, smoothed by many rains and covered with green moss. The stones were laid out in orderly rows, and suddenly we realised that we were walking on graves. For a moment we stood quite still, and then looked up the hill. We saw a big cemetery with hundreds of graves all crowded together, big and small. We were startled and remained silent. To our right stretched a rich valley, and here we were, walking on graves, forgotten graves. Death was all round us. A cemetery on the hill, and water which made a man's belly swell, in the valley. The evil spirit of the place had already killed two previous villages. And the swamps surrounded us, black and cruel. Then the youngest of our group whispered, 'We are glad to be alive, aren't we?'

'Then we will settle here!' rejoined his comrade.

Somebody else suggested a plan for draining the swamp. The memory of Hadera and the swamps there came back to us. As we went down the hill, we all knew that here was where we would build our moshav.

At the beginning the Emek was quite empty of settlement. The only signs of life were a few scattered villages on the distant hills, with sheep and goats grazing near the muddy wells. Every so often shepherds would pump up some water, empty it into the clay drinking troughs, and stretch out under the trees again.

Twenty of us had set up a little camp of seven tents on a hill by the Arab village, built on the slopes of the white mountain. In the most prominent position among our tents was a kind of square hut with matting walls. This was our kitchen and dining hall. From the hill-top one could see deserted trenches dating from Turkish days. Below us was the Government road. Night fell and the moon was bright in the sky. Suddenly somebody noticed that the white horse was missing. Many of our group were already asleep in our tents, so only a few of us could go and look for the horse. We found him in the village storehouse.

At sunrise two carts arrived at the site. The drivers and their companions got out and began to climb towards our camp. Everyone was wrapped in his own thoughts and conversation had petered out. Gradually, determination replaced uncertainty in our hearts, though deep down, a little doubt still nagged at us. Then the men arrived at our camp and we collected together some stones and made a table for them for our first repast in our village.

Even before the first settlers moved to the site the surveyors were there, measuring out the land so that the necessary maps and plans could be drawn up correctly. They would start work early in the morning, taking their equipment from the big store-room in the village, and clambering up to the hill-tops to take their sights and make their measurements.

We regarded this survey as one of the most important preparatory stages and we spent relatively large sums of money on it. The surveyors were still at work when we moved on to the site permanently, and were continually surprising us with the results of their observations. We had always thought that the Shimron spring was at a much lower level than the village, and it looked as if it was. But the surveyors told us that it was fifty feet or so higher, and that the water would flow down on to our land without our needing to pump it, so saving us a major item of expenditure. Thanks to the survey, we were able to save the cost of two bridges when we built our approach road, because we knew the height of the ground at various spots. The knowledge gained from the survey also enabled us to build irrigation and drainage channels for the water from the different springs in such a way that no pumping was needed, as the water flowed along the channels by gravity, irrigating large areas of land. Finally, our plans for building our village were based on this survey.

The days passed, and here I was covering the ground between the Government road and our camp for the third time. Our light tents and the big matting-walled hut were clearly visible on the hill top, and three of us were making our way there from the railway—myself, laden with bundles, my six-year old son, and his mother. It was a long way and we sweated profusely. We stopped for a moment and looked around us. This was where the settlement would be, but how would we build it and when?

The hill was the first spot we settled. We cleared it of dirt, uprooted the bushes and the thorns, and pitched our tents in an orderly group, with a trench all round them for defence.

From the hill-top with its fresh, cool air we could see everything that went on in the valley, and look out on all our land. At night we used to think about our new way of life—the conquest of the soil!

We who lived in the eight tents were the first twenty. We worked hard right from the beginning, helping with the surveying, marking out the limits of the swamps, clearing the land of stones, doing guard duty, bringing barrels of water from the village and bread from Haifa, this last often taking two days. We wanted to decide exactly how we were going to establish our settlement, and the order of work. Our comrades came to the hill-top on foot, by cart and by train from all over the country, and we had our first general meeting in a large tent specially erected for the purpose.

Our first general meeting took place in September, 1921 on the Hill of Conquest and lasted 3 days. This was really Nahalal's foundation meeting, and many of the people there, who did not even know each other at the time, were destined to be among the builders of Nahalal. After having elected our first village council with seven members, the meeting went on to consider the fundamental principles on which our settlement would be based, among them living by our own labour, speaking only Hebrew, and helping each other in times of need.

In the course of time our membership grew to eighty. The new members were chosen either because they volunteered to join us of their own accord or because they were recommended by existing members. The rules for setting up a workers' settlement specified that new members could only be elected and approved at a general meeting of existing members, and that was where the problem lay. Who was to elect whom, and how? The meeting decided that the best way to settle the question was for everyone at the meeting to vote on everyone else by secret ballot. Anyone with ten or more votes against him would not remain a member, because he would only be a source of friction and dispute. Everyone at the meeting was elected, and nobody received anything like ten votes against.

We all knew that we were going to build our permanent home on a small hill in the centre of our fields. Every member would receive a small plot of ground next to his house for growing vegetables. We could not decide whether to move our temporary camp there or leave it where it was. Winter was coming, and if we were going to move camp we ought to do so quickly. On the other hand, the small hill was surrounded by swampy ground and if we moved there we might get malaria.

Many meetings were held on the subject without arriving at a decision. Doctors and sanitary engineers investigated and expressed their doubts of the wisdom of moving, friends came to give their advice, senior officials of various institutions counselled us against it. In the end, as if driven by some inner compulsion, we did move, two months after we had first erected our tents on the 'Hill of Conquest'. The small hill in the centre of our fields, where we put up our tents again, is today still the centre of our village.

The rainy season began with heavy downpours, but whenever the rain stopped we busied ourselves with various building jobs— breaking up stones for gravel, digging trenches as a defence against surprise attacks, putting up a sandbag redoubt, and digging drainage channels.

Although all these were essential jobs, they did not satisfy us. We wanted to plough and to sow, not break stones. The land was in a sorry state too, most of it swampy, stony and covered with thorns and bushes, though here and there plants were sprouting. It was just crying out to be ploughed and sown. From the political point of view as well it was essential to start ploughing, at least on the boundaries, because the Arabs were ploughing right up to and beyond them.

One bright very sunny morning, the first after many days of cold, rain and mud, three pairs of mules went out to plough. Groups of us gathered round each plough, all of us putting a hand on it somewhere, so that we could all feel that we were taking part in the turning of the first furrow on our new land.

The ploughman just ploughed up the land on our boundaries and we sowed it with seed. However, we did not want to restrict our sowing to this in case of disputes with the Arabs, so we scattered some seed here and there on the rest of the land. It was only at the end of the sowing season, however, that we managed to plough some of the smaller fields in the centre of our land and sow them. We could not do more because we were short of mules.

Even while we were still on the Hill of Conquest comrades from outside came along and asked to join us, and now many more came and our numbers grew. Every new member had to be authorised by the committee, which gave its authorisation according to the state of our budget and our work. There was plenty of work for everybody, building the road and digging drainage channels, but accommodation was a problem because there were not enough tents to house families with young children. From the security point of view, this was no place to bring young children either. In addition to twenty of the original members, therefore, there were only a few others actually living on the site. The women and children had to live elsewhere. Some were at Merhavia but most were at Nazareth, the administrative town of the region, an hour's walk along the mountain paths from where we were.

All the families lived together in one large house in the Arab town for eight months. They organised a kindergarten in the house, and hardly went out of doors at all. Once or twice a week, particularly on Saturdays, we used to go into Nazareth to see how our families were and to tell them what we had done during the week, and consult with them about further work on our village and our private plots of land. We missed our families terribly and they missed us, but the worst affected of all were the women. They had no chance at all to participate in the preliminary work of establishing and building our new settlement, which was to be based on equal rights and responsibilities for men and women from the very beginning.

Devora was pregnant again, and being weak and ill needed me more than ever.

November 2nd, 1921 was a day of special concern for all of us. We were afraid of Arab attacks, as this was the fourth anniversary of the Balfour Declaration. Accordingly half of us went to Nazareth to be with the women and children, and half of us stayed at home in our camp.

There were a few black tents on the hillside above the Simonia spring at the approaches to Nazareth. Most of the tent-dwellers were women and children, although there were a few men among them. The tents were almost entirely hidden by the trees growing round the pond formed by the spring, so it was almost as if they were not there at all.

When we first came to the area the people who lived in the tents gave us angry looks and greeted us with sullen silence. They were not peasants and would not demean themselves by working on the land, so why did they look at us like that?

The land was stony and thorny, but we worked hard at clearing it, and as the piles of stones grew the area of clear land increased, and it did our hearts good to see it.

By the trees near the spring there was a steeply sloping hill, covered with rocks and stones. The ground between them, what could be seen of it at least, was white and dry because of the lime in it. Vegetation grew thickly there, but at the first signs of summer it withered and died. From the hill-top one could see the whole Emek, and in the summer a cooling wind blew there. To the west of the hill were the burial grounds of earlier settlements, their gravestones smoothed by the rain and eaten away by time.

As we worked away at clearing our land we found many big, round, smooth stones that must have been pillars of some kind at one time, and after a great deal of hard work we uncovered the remains of walls and small chambers. The ground all round us was littered with potsherds. To the east was the almost vertical hill, rocky and completely uncultivable, and on the other side of it, almost at its foot, were the ruins of the ancient synagogue of Simonia, discovered by archaeologists and then covered up again so that no evil eye should have dominion over it.

In the winter we all climbed the hill, determined to conquer it and make its soil fruitful. We cut down the tall grass with sickles, breaking not a few of them on the moss-grown stones scattered on the ground. We turned the ground over, planted gourd seeds and brought up cans to water them with. We got quite good crops.

We concentrated on the hill and its surroundings, sowing, ploughing, digging out lime deposits and removing stones. This was the hardest job of all, because some of the stones were so big and heavy that they took days to remove and needed several people to get them on to the carts to be taken away.

Gradually the whole place began to look different. We uprooted the thorns and the weeds, and uncovered good clear land. The Arabs in the black tents moved further in among the trees, and we had no contact with them at all. They tended their flocks and left the land alone. Relations with them were correct but distant.

Devora gave birth to our daughter in Haifa, and after a period in hospital joined us in Nahalal. We were a family of four now.

We had moved onto our land against the advice of Dr. Hillel Jaffé, the well-known friend of all workers, and despite the misgivings of our friends. Nevertheless we had not forgotten what had happened to the settlers of Hadera and Yesod Hama'aleh—most of them had contracted malaria. We knew that drainage work was the first essential, and the Jewish National Fund had given us a grant for this purpose. We had retained the Histadrut company, 'Building and Public Works Office' (the forerunner of Solel Boneh), to do the job, but the supervising engineer ran into difficulties. The Arabs would not allow any digging on their land, one of the reasons being that they watered their flocks in the swamps. They did not confine themselves to vocal opposition but ruined a great deal of the work. The Government authorities were as bad. In the end we managed to come to terms with our neighbours, installing water pipes for them inside our boundaries, and then they and the authorities left us alone.

The Nahalal drainage project was the first of its kind in Palestine, and cost tens of thousands of pounds. Three or four hundred employees of the Histadrut company worked on it for a year, aided by some of our members. There were only a few of them, and our group was sad because other hands than ours were preparing our land for settlement, but we consoled ourselves with the thought that this was the only way to make the place habitable and healthy quickly, and reduce the chances of catching malaria. As it was, during the summer of 1922, our first summer at Nahalal, ten per cent of us were going down with malaria every month. A year later this had been reduced to one per cent.

Not only was the anopheles mosquito—and hence malaria—almost entirely eliminated by the draining of the swamps, but we were able to use the water which had once caused the deaths of so many people. We used it to irrigate 500 dunams of land, and also piped the water of the Shimron spring to every house at Nahalal. Not only that, but we reclaimed 3,550 dunams of swampland and cultivated it, obtaining extremely good crops.

In 1924 a doctor examined everyone in the village. He said: 'Here, man has triumphed over Nature and death'. He was right.

So far we had paved only about a mile and a half of the road we wanted to build from the Government road to our land. It took a day to bring materials from Haifa to where our road began—a distance of eighteen miles—and another hard day's work to transport them the rest of the way from where our road ended to the fields. We sank in mud up to our knees, often losing our boots, and the mules staggered and stumbled as they tried to take the weight of the carts. Often we used to stop the carts where they were, and unload them piecemeal, making our way laboriously through the mud, and often falling and becoming filthy from head to foot. Sometimes we had to abandon carts completely, because they were so firmly stuck in the mud that nothing would move them. It was impossible to start building, or indeed do any ploughing or sowing, without a road along which to bring implements and working animals and supplies. We asked the J. N. F. for help, but they refused it at first. Some of our members thought them right, saying that the Fund must devote all its money to redeeming the soil, and none could be spared to help us pay for building a road. In the end, however, we did receive financial assistance and engaged for the job the same Histadrut company which had carried out our drainage work. After some months the road was finished, but we discovered in the course of time that the basalt rocks we had used were not really suitable.

Several pairs of strong mules were harnessed behind each other, with the strongest pair leading. Each pair of mules was yoked together and a chain ran from each yoke to another chain, a long thick one stretching from the first pair of mules to the plough itself, a heavy one which ploughed a furrow some nineteen to twenty-four inches deep.

Two men guided the plough, and there was a man at the head of each pair of mules, urging them on with much shouting and cracking of the whip. Slowly the teams moved forward, and as the ploughshare bit into the ground it turned over great clods of earth like waves on the sea. Soil that had lain as if dead for years was bared to the sun and the wind and brought to life. It was poor soil, however, light in colour and poor in yield. It would have to be prepared and strengthened before it would yield the crops we wanted. There was manure to spare in the neighbouring villages. It had been piled up there for scores, if not hundreds of years, and it was by the manure heaps that the villagers used to hold their public meetings, or just stand and talk. We took this manure by the hundreds of cartloads and dumped it on our land. It was black, well-rotted, fine and light, and we scattered it from the carts by hand, covering the fields and giving them an entirely new aspect. Then we took the carts to the steep hill where the soil was all lime, filled them, and put lime on the ground also. We dug it all well in, and ploughed it again. When we had established our dairy cattle sheds we had our own supply of manure, and this too we spread on the land. Everything we planted grew thick and green and strong, and the land became once more, what it ought always to have been—rich and bountiful and responsive to cultivation.

Once harvesting ends, the life goes out of the fields. The stubble is ploughed in, and the bare soil lies in great clods under the sky. The maize has all been picked and only the stalks are left, rows and rows of them, their leaves flapping in the wind. Goats pick their way among them, looking for bits to eat.

Days grew shorter and nights colder. Clouds appeared in the sky and in the afternoons a brisk wind arose, heralding winter. The trees in the garden begin to shed their leaves, gradually carpeting the ground all around them. The vegetable garden needed less water and the fruit trees were not watered at all. Tractors prepared the fields for sowing, and the tempo of work slowed down a little.

In the summer, everything had been left out in the open—hay, straw, sacks of grain, maize stalks, empty sacks, and so on. Now everything was put under cover, because the light rain that usually falls at the time of the Feast of Tabernacles warned us that winter's downpours would soon be here.

When the rainy season starts, the weather grows cooler and there is already a feeling of winter in the air. The soil soaks up the rain and becomes easier to work. We could start breaking it up and hoeing it ready for manuring and sowing.

The year's work came to an end. We had done what we had to do, and the land was ready. As the days shortened we finished work earlier and could relax at home in the evenings.

The night is bright and starry. The ploughman greases his plough and his cart, feeds and waters his mule, and rubs her down ready for the day's sowing ahead. Then, his son or some other members helping him, he makes ready seed, chemical fertiliser, his ploughshare, his whip, and water and food for himself and his mule. Then he lies down to sleep, tired but content, to prepare himself for the day that lies ahead.

At dawn he loads everything onto the cart, (the plough and the seed drill have already been secured behind the cart), drinks a glass of tea, climbs onto the cart, and sets off. The cart clatters across the yard, the driver sitting on sacks of seed and holding the reins loosely in his hand. On the way he is joined by other carts, their drivers muffled in heavy coats, all bound for the fields.

Mist covers the face of the earth. The morning dew makes everything moist and fresh. The skies are dark and cloudy, and the fields stretch out ahead, smooth and level.

The sower strides out, taking the seed from an open sack slung low across the left side of his chest, and scatters it on the soil. After him comes his son with the plough, cutting long, straight furrows and covering the seed. There is rain in the air, and we all have only one thought in our minds—to finish sowing before the rain starts. The sower strides powerfully on, hot and sweating with exertion, but determined to bring his task to a successful conclusion.

Everywhere one looks, there are men sowing seed in the rich, dark soil, and ploughing the seed into the ground. We are obeying Nature's laws and united in toil, a symbol of a working nation, tilling its own soil.

Thunder and lightning usually announce the beginning of the rainy season, and when the rain comes it falls in big heavy drops. The plants and the trees drink it thirstily as the soil soaks it up, and every crevice and cranny of the ground is filled with water. The garden has been watered all summer, and its soil is not as dry as the fields. They soak up every drop of rain as it falls, and the two inches or so with which the rainy season usually opens are not enough to quench their thirst.

All day and night it rains without a stop. The soil becomes waterlogged and muddy; the rain pouring down the hillsides and slopes cuts little channels which are full to overflowing. The rain drums on the roof and runs down the windows. It keeps everyone inside, men, women and children. When anyone does go outside, there is mud everywhere. It is no good wearing shoes because they will let in water, so gumboots are the order of the day. The man of the house cannot work in the fields, so he stays indoors with a book.

In the intervals between downpours the whole family goes out to plant beets, but even if the rain does not hold off for long they work on, getting soaked but not wanting to leave their work half done. Very often too, one has to fill a bucket with water for the mule, and wade through the mud with it to the stable. Water pipes have not yet been installed there, and in this weather the mules refuse to go out to the water troughs.

The weather is like this for ten to fifteen days in the winter, but things are somewhat easier the rest of the time because there are short periods when the rain stops altogether. Then the men of the settlement work at repairing their tools and farming implements, catch up with office work, do the accounts, and work in the stores and barns. But there is not too much to do on a winter's day, and when it is raining one can sit at home with a glass of tea, or stretch out on the couch and read, or make up for sleep lost during the summer.

By the end of February the wild flowers are growing in the fields and on the mountain-sides. The children bring home great bunches of them that they have picked on their walks. Men and trees shake off the thrall of winter. The garden round the house is dug over and flowers planted. The women sow summer vegetables in the kitchen gardens. The sun is growing stronger and invites us all to warm ourselves in its rays. The goatherds take the goats into the fields, and the women drive the cows and calves out of the yard.

Later, when the ground has dried out a little, the villagers start ploughing ready for the summer crops. The first leaves have begun to grow on the vines; the beets, in long green rows, have begun to sprout; the little cucumbers are growing too, and the potato plants are tall and covered with white flowers; the fields set aside for melons and maize—to be used for fodder—are all ready for sowing. All round lies the greens and black chequerboard of the fields.

At the end of the day, work over, you go home, play with the children, and afterwards when they are in bed lie down with them for a while, before going into your own room to sit at the window and look at the moon and hear the birds singing, while in the distance you can hear the last cart rumbling home, returning late from the fields.

The village awakes early in the summer. The women set about milking the cows, the warm smell of the milk mingling with the sharp tang of cow-dung. The men make their way to the dairy with

G

the churns, the milk is weighed, the amount noted and the churns emptied. The carts begin trundling out of the yards on their way to the fields. In an hour, everything is silent. The men are working in the fields, the women are busy in the houses and yards, and the children are at school. At noon the carts return from the fields and the cows are taken into the cowshed for the midday milking.

On any summer's afternoon there are scores of carts standing near the produce sheds, having brought fruit and vegetables of all kinds for grading, weighing, packing and despatch to the towns and cities. At one o'clock the family sits down to eat, and then there is silence in the house for two or three hours as everyone settles down for a rest before going back to work. Outside not a soul can be seen.

The harvest season is approaching. In the yards the machinery is being got ready. Tall frames are built round the sides of the carts so that they will hold more when reaping starts, and everyone lends a hand with bringing home the harvest. Here and there harvesting has already begun. The whole family sets to, the farmer, his wife and his children, and everything else is put aside until harvesting is done. Work goes on from early morning until far into the night. Threshing is done simultaneously with harvesting. When the carts have been piled high with grain they make their way to one of the grain stores in the village where the threshing machine has been installed, and twenty or thirty villagers working at the threshing machine together, unload the carts and put their loads through the machine.

Harvesting and threshing last a full month. The members of the settlement divide themselves up into three or four groups and each group chooses its foreman. Then they work at top speed for the month until the grain has all been harvested and threshed. When it is all finished they bring cakes, wine, grapes and melons and celebrate another harvest home, sitting among the sacks of grain spread on the granary floor.

Cattle suffer from many diseases, but the worst is contagious abortion. Some say that this was introduced into the country by the first cows imported from Holland, but this cannot be so, for a certain farm with Dutch cows has never had a single outbreak, whereas serious outbreaks have occurred at other farms a long way from that one. Nobody really knows where the disease came from and how it started.

One day we saw that many of our cows were sick. One after the other they aborted, so that there were no calves and the milk yield dwindled. The illness spread and the whole village was threatened. Everybody was afraid to visit his neighbour's farm in case he took the disease back to his own cattle. Nobody sold a cow if he could possibly avoid it, and those who had to sell were forced to do so at pitifully low prices.

Our losses mounted and we were faced with a situation where the main pillar of our economy—our cattle and our dairy—seemed on the point of total collapse. We held out. Experts said that nothing could be done to eradicate the disease. In some countries, Holland for instance, the disease had existed for years. The Government and various institutions had tried to stamp it out, but without success. All that we could do, they said, was to dispose of all our cows, leave the cowsheds empty for one or two years, dig up the ground inside them and in the yard to a depth of three feet, and spray the ground and the sheds themselves. Even then there was no certainty that the disease would not break out again.

The owners of the sick cows said that they could not possibly dispose of their cows. After many meetings it was finally decided that if the cows had to be disposed of, then everybody would have to contribute towards compensation for the farmers concerned, not only for the low prices their cows would fetch, but also for the income they would lose until they replaced their cows with others.

The position was serious and we were filled with doubt about what to do, because there were other experts who counselled against disposing of our cattle. In the meantime, the village had got into grave economic straits. We were heavily in debt, both privately and collectively, and our produce was fetching very low prices. The discussions were long and bitter and a great deal of tact was needed to persuade the owners of the sick cattle to dispose of them. Then we tried a difficult experiment in mutual aid, and we succeeded.

First we borrowed several thousand pounds (in those days a huge amount of money). Then we erected a special shed where all the sick cows were kept until they could be sold, and where they were looked after by one man. Meanwhile we paid the full price for each cow to its owner immediately we took it over, together with compensation for his loss of income. At the same time, we took healthy cows from other farmers and gave them to the less lucky ones whose cows were sick. In addition we took all the other measures we had been advised to take, like spraying, and deep digging in the yards.

All these operations were conducted by a committee we had all elected, and to whom we had given full powers. There could be appeals against its decisions, to an appeals committee we had also elected, and the decisions of the appeals committee were final and binding.

This had been a difficult time from every point of view—economic, financial, organisational and social—but we came through it successfully. Since then there has been no further outbreak of contagious abortion at Nahalal. Milk yields have risen and our cattle and dairy have gone from strength to strength, bringing prosperity to the village.

At first there were those among us who thought that it was impossible for us to lead a life without books and without spiritual sustenance. But did we want to have intellectuals in our settlement as well? 'No,' was the answer at the time. 'We must turn from our previous ways of life and create a nation of workers on the land. The pioneer settlers who chose this path succeeded. They created a new way of life, a new people's culture, a culture of fields and gardens, of economic independence. This may not sound very reassuring, but there is no escaping the fact that our achievements in the field of culture have by no means been small. We have created a new way of life for our people, we have produced a whole agricultural and social literature, we have made laws and customs to regulate our conduct.'

And yet, in our hearts, we often felt that something was lacking. We wanted to be united in thought with a world other than ours, we wanted to give artistic expression to our feeling, we wanted to share in the questionings and controversies of the world at large. But the answer lay with us. For years we had continued in the same old way, every now and again deciding that we needed a richer cultural life but doing nothing about it. Not that we wish to pretend that we saw in our life something far superior to any other, but the brute fact is that ten or twelve hours of work a day demand bodily strength and spiritual strength alike, and leave a man no strength to spare for anything else. Our work and achievements are as good as those of farmers in other countries who have been on the land for generations. In a short time we have succeeded in the most difficult undertaking of all for a people cut off from the land and all feeling for it for thousands of years. Books are being published, plays written, pictures painted—the range of cultural activity in the world is vast. But we have no time to savour it. Our working day is too long and hard and tiring, and rural life is physically too exacting to leave us time or strength to read.

There is another reason too. We cannot afford to devote any time to culture when we could be working and earning. We work at a fast pace, not by chance but because we must. We hunger to produce goods, not so that we may amass more property as a result, but so that we can develop our economy. When we farm ever more intensively we do not do so in order to make more profits, but to increase still more the number of settlements and the population they will support. That is why every day is too short, why we get up with the sun and work till after sunset.

If this is the fate of all workers on the land, how much more so is it our fate, for we have had to start from the beginning and build from nothing. We have come now towards the evening of our lives, and even if we seem to be losing so much that we can never regain, we have no choice—we must press on along our chosen path. We are building a mighty edifice, and the pace is too fast for us to be able to spare any effort to live a complete and tranquil spiritual life.

All this is not to say that nobody at Nahalal ever reads anything. Most people take a daily paper. There is a well stocked library, and all our members do a great deal of reading during the autumn and winter evenings. Our children and youth read a tremendous amount, and most people subscribe to technical and literary journals and party publications. All this, however, is not always enough for people's spiritual needs.

A working man looks forward to Saturday, the Sabbath, the day of rest. He can relax, sit about, lie down, read, go for a walk. In the spring he can sit in his garden and enjoy the trees and the flowers. As we are not religious in any way the Sabbath is not a time of prayer for us, and the festivals have no religious content as far as we are concerned. At Passover, for instance, we do not have the traditional Seder, with its reading from the Haggada about the exodus from Egypt, or the various dishes symbolising the sufferings of the Israelites in Egypt, or the recital of prayers, or the opening of the door for the prophet Elijah, because we do not believe in any of it.

But we do have a celebration. Everything is decorated with flowers and we buy new clothes for the children. Everyone invites relatives and friends, and in the big hall the tables are covered with white tablecloths. There are flowers on the tables, and there is wine. All cares are forgotten and the hall is full of friendly talk.

But in the midst of all the merriment something dies in one's heart, and the pleasures of the celebration vanish like stars disappearing one by one from the sky. One sits there disappointed, like a man bereft of all feelings of devotion, as if dawn is breaking and shattering the magic of the night.

At Shavuot (Pentecost) we bring the first fruits of our fields and gardens as an offering to the Jewish National Fund. The children decorate farm carts and horses, and load them with sheaves of wheat and barley, beets, gourds, vegetables of all kinds, bunches of grapes, young chicks and white doves. Then they deck themselves with green branches and garland their heads with flowers. As the carts pass through the village all the villagers join up with them singing as they go. Then the carts of the other villages, also accompanied by children and grown-ups, join the procession, and at the assembly hall the first fruits are handed over by the children, to the accompaniment of singing and chanting.

The rain drums endlessly on the low hut's metal roof. It is early morning now and he will not be able to fall asleep again. He lies there, smoking and thinking, reviewing his life. What a difference between the active, independent life he had once lived in the town and his idle, useless life here.

He had always been rebellious from the very beginning, when he refused to follow the custom of the men of his family and become a shochet (ritual slaughterer). He opened a shop instead, with a partner, and spent the best years of his youth worrying, calculating, trying to cope with mountains of bills. Knowing almost nothing about business, he eventually lost everything he had.

Because they trusted him, the merchants of the town commissioned him to do their buying for them in the country town, and he used to go and order there the cloth they needed for their businesses, earning a little money by this means. But hard as he worked, he still could not earn enough to support his family.

On Sundays Rav Avraham used to make the rounds of the shops, taking orders and writing them in his notebook, and collecting samples, letters to big merchants in the city, and money to pay for the cloth. On Monday evening Ivan the carter took Rav Avraham to the city, driving his cart all through the night to reach there by morning.

Rav Avraham could not make ends meet, so he decided to go to Odessa, taking his family with him. It was winter time, and they made the journey by horse and cart, all eight of them. In Odessa they lived in a basement room, which also served as Avraham's business premises, for he now sold bits of pastry and a few items of grocery. Little Moshele had to be taken to hospital, and never returned. The children could not study, and apart from that, Rav Avraham had to keep his 'shop' open on Saturdays. So they all went back to their own town.

Perhaps it was because of their desperately hard living conditions that his sons rebelled and left home. They were the only ones in the whole area to do so. They must have had a prophetic vision and known what was coming, because they certainly left at the right moment.

He remembered their leaving. Would he ever forget it? It had been morning, and Ivan's cart had been standing outside. Half the town had been there to see them off. They had put their belongings on the cart and it had moved off. Everyone had cried, and the tears had still been running down their faces when the cart had disappeared in the distance. Rav Avraham and his wife stayed behind and waited for their letters, the only pleasure left. Then came the War, and they were cut off from all contact for four years. After the War there were revolutions and pogroms. The town was burnt down and the Jews ran away to Rumania, taking only the clothes they stood up in.

Eventually Rav Avraham arrived in Tel Aviv. Once again he

wanted to be independent and earn his own living, so he opened a tiny grocery shop in the suburbs. But his strength gave out and he could not run the shop any longer, so his sons took him to the village of Nahalal to live.

There he saw how they lived, two sons and two daughters, all of them farmers, working hard all day and in the evenings, and not even resting properly on Saturdays. And what did they have to show for it? Poverty! It was the same as in Russia in the old days, the old man thought to himself. True, they were never pampered. But then, what pleasure have I had in my life? And what have I given them? Still, nothing like this ever happened in my family before. But they believe in a world to come of their own, Zionism, and it seems good to them. And what have we, the few parents they have collected here like ears of corn?

It was already morning. Rav Avraham's son was already bringing home the milk. Rav Avraham wrapped himself in his prayer shawl, and Haya, the mother of his children, also joined in his quick prayer, putting on her glasses and opening the prayerbook in the lamplight. She listened to Rav Avraham intoning the prayers and her cares fell from her. She was full of hope now, looking forward to their grandchildren's visit, when everyone would be gay. She would give them nuts and raisins when they came.

And Rav Avraham was thinking about the crops and calculating the income to be expected from every one of them. In the synagogue—the old people's club—they would argue about their sons and how well they worked and the prospects of Zionism.

But no. It was not the same synagogue, nor the same congregation, nor the same feeling. The company of old people and their conversation were difficult to bear, and he could not really participate in his sons' conversations, which were always about what was happening in the country. Something had broken inside Rav Avraham, and it would not soon mend again.

The sun is setting, sinking into the sea beyond Mount Carmel. The shadows of the mountains lengthen in the valley. I am tired in every limb and stretch out on the ground to rest.

There stands the modest little house, newly built and shining white. Building materials lie scattered about, but soon they will all be cleared away and the house will be ready for occupation. Behind the house stands a wooden hut, with cracked walls, and its foundation stones lying higgledy-piggledy all round it. The hut is full of life, with children playing noisily inside and their mother trying to quieten them, promising: 'Tomorrow, we'll move from here into the house'.

As I lie there on my back looking up at the sky I remember other days, days without a house, when we did not feel the lack of one. They were good days, when even to think of having a house was considered akin to arrogance. What do these people who live in houses know of true happiness? Here in Palestine they have the chance of living a life which has abolished individual needs, a life where a man does not live for himself alone, but finds his pleasure in the general pleasure. One by one I can recall all the different kinds of living accommodation I have had during my thirty years in the country.

The first was a hut in the mother of settlements, Petach Tikva. There were and are many fine houses in Petach Tikva, but then I was an unemployed working man, so I sought out a mouldering little hut near the workers' library. I had malaria and was running a temperature of more than 104°, and the hut was so stifling that I almost fainted from the stuffy heat.

Then there was the watchman's hut in the vineyards at Rehovot, the walls made of sacking and mats sewn together. It was a wonderful summer residence!

Later there was a small wooden hut near the road to Ein Ganim, with a path that came out near Sejja, an Arab village. This hut was a lively place, a kind of hostel, with a constantly changing population. People passing through used to spend the night there, workers seeking jobs congregated there, and it was a haunt of writers and various party members.

The public hut at Kfar Saba was just as lively. We slept and ate there, stored our tools there, used it as a labour exchange and held meetings there. On Saturday nights workers from Petach Tikva used to arrive there barefoot, and with a week's supply of bread and coconut oil in their haversacks. On Friday afternoon they would set off for Petach Tikva again to spend Saturday there.

At Hadera, in the Dorshei Zion orange grove, there was a ruined house, the only building. By day we worked hard in the grove and by night we had to keep a look-out for thieves.

At Yavniel I slept in the stable, together with the mules. In the morning I fed them, greased the cart ready for use and drank a glass of hot tea. Then I brushed down the mules, harnessed them to the cart, and set off for my work in the fields just as the sleepy settlement was coming to life.

And then there was Kinneret, where I slept in a welter of plough-shares and harrows and seed drills. A little later I slept in the motor room for a few months, where the first thing I saw when I awoke was the huge flywheel of the petrol engine, waiting to be started up for the day's work.

Later at Um-Juni there were a few scattered clay houses by the stormy, swift-flowing Jordan. We built two wooden huts there. One was a two-storey building, with our dining hall downstairs and living accommodation upstairs, while the second was for the mules. The fodder was piled high there, and we slept in among it warm and comfortable. When the stars came out we used to get up and sow our fields across the Jordan with wheat—the seed of bread, the seed of hope.

And when the houses were built at Degania—two-storey houses—we did not want to leave our beds of straw. Our transfer to the houses was carried out without enthusiasm. The first people to move into them were the new members who had not been in the country long and had not had the chance of finding out how good it was to be without a house.

Then came the dark days of the first World War under Turkish rule. We lived in a hay loft without doors or windows, crowded and cramped together. But still, in our dark living quarters we managed to keep a spark of our ideals alive. Not for ourselves only, but for those who were to come after. Then the darkness lifted, war ended and with fresh strength we resumed the building of our country.

Next we moved into our new accommodation—army tents. Army tents were valuable possessions and played an important part in our movement. A tent was a very comfortable place to live in. Many were the babies who spent their first months in one. Dining room, bedroom, guest room and work room combined, a tent was easy to move and put up somewhere else when necessary.

On the Hill of Conquest we lived in tents again, bought this time from the Egyptian army. Whenever stormy winds blew on a dark winter's night, they would collapse and it was no easy matter to put them up again.

In the spring we built wooden huts and roofed them over with branches, covering the door and window openings with reeds. Here our children were born and grew up. In the winter we moved our huts to more level ground, built another room on to them and covered the roof with flattened paraffin cans. A year went by, two years, and then we managed to obtain some army surplus planks and boards which we used to make floors for our huts. We added kitchens, and then we had really good living accommodation.

The years passed, our families grew, we were weakened by illness. After fifteen years our huts began to disintegrate. The wind began to whistle through their walls and they leaked. In stormy weather they rocked like a ship at sea. In the end the time came to move to a proper house, a house built of stone standing among the now full-grown trees, a house for our children and our children's children. Will it be lived in by them all? Our lives are short, and we want to postpone their ending.

Eighty plots of ground at Nahalal were divided into eight zones with a path running across each one to the fields. Each zone was allocated a supply of the larger implements—harrows, rakes, mowers and the like—for the collective use of all the members who lived in that particular zone. When there was a second distribution of land, people who lived next door to each other in a zone did not necessarily have their fields next to one another, so the paths cutting across each zone were reduced to an absolute minimum. In the meantime implements had been broken or damaged, or had been exchanged for others, so bigger general partnerships grew up in the use of the remainder. Everything came to be done on a larger scale and eventually the zones themselves just merged. The only things that remained the same were the communal grain stores, one to each zone. They are still used to this day for threshing maize.

At the beginning there were many attempts to combine into large groups and farm together. Old-timers from Upper and Lower Galilee who settled in one of the zones, some of them the sons and daughters of farmers, tried to form one such group.

They knew each other's ways of working, they knew the country, they knew each other's customs and language, and they thought that these factors would make a larger grouping both easy and worthwhile. Half the farmers of zone D, who had come from Kibbutz Merhavia and afterwards founded Kibbutz Geva, also wanted to combine in a large group. They worked together for a short while but then they split up again and went back to working their own individual fields. Only two families, who had lived together for some years before coming to Nahalal because the wives were sisters, managed to set up a real commune and live a completely communal life.

But even individualistic Nahalal has not rejected completely all ideas of partnership and co-operation, particularly in matters connected with the members' daily work. There is full co-operation in the use of ploughs and other implements, hand-tools, carts, reapers, and work animals, both between individuals and between groups.

There are many items of equipment and machinery which belong to the village as a whole, such as tractors, threshing machines and pumps, and the village owns collectively all the wells, springs, ponds and pipelines. All equipment, machinery, pipelines, and so on are supervised by the village council, but villagers still feel individual responsibility for them, especially for the machinery and implements.

Apart from this there are also the village's collective enterprises —the dairy, the breeding station, the flour mill, the produce marketing organisation, transport and others. Most of them are run by a management elected from among the villagers, and are in large measure responsible for the way of life and work of all the members of the village, and perpetuate the feeling of general co-operation. This entire collective economy has an appreciable influence on every member's private economic situation. The collective nature of such institutions as loan funds, found everywhere else as well, is more strongly felt at Nahalal.

There were children among the first families to settle at Nahalal, so we were occupied with the question of education from the very beginning.

One evening there was a tap on the entrance to the tent and a bespectacled young man entered. He was dressed in a Russian shirt, with a fringed belt tied round his middle, was well-groomed, and had a smile on his face. He was a candidate for the post of teacher. He was the same age as the settlers, and wholeheartedly believed in free, informal education. He was ready to take on the task of educating the young generation and was prepared to accept condidions as they were.

A small wooden hut was erected for the school and Meshoulam Halevy presided ever it. There was magic in the man. He was modest and restrained in his ways and in his speech, and he loved the children, who loved him in return, whatever their age. They played all round him and followed him wherever he went, because he understood them.

He controlled his classes perfectly. A word, a smile or a hint of dissatisfaction were enough to curb a child who was being naughty or disturbing the rest of the class. His lessons always captured their interest, for he was an expert on every subject, particularly poetry, music and painting. Children and grown-ups alike formed a choir and an orchestra, and the whole village enjoyed their performances.

As the number of children grew we had to take on more teachers, and each one brought his own methods. Every teacher was given his own class, and if at any time any of them tried to teach any class but his own there were outcries and objections, and so much noise that one could not hear oneself speak. As the years went by there were all kinds of troubles, but even intervention by various educational institutes did not help. As is usual in these cases, the difficult individuals became parents in their turn. Some supported one teacher, others another. Public opinion was split, so everyone suffered, especially the teachers.

After some years the Education Centre decided to put an end to all the bitter controversies. New teachers were brought in, and the old ones had to leave.

The village school's curriculum today is the usual one for rural schools as drawn up by the Education Centre. Children from four to six years of age attend the kindergarten section. From six to fourteen they go to school full time, and then have half-day lessons for a further two years. The school is the first charge on the village's budget and everybody pays an equal amount towards it, whether there are children in the family or not.

The village committee is the body responsible for all village affairs, except economic matters normally dealt with by the economic institutions, and is the enforcement body for all decisions of the general council and village general meetings. The committee is responsible for education, medical aid, mutual help, the organisation of guard duties, dealings with all Government departments and other outside bodies or individuals. The committee is also responsible for roads, school buildings, the communal hall, and so on. What local taxes shall be levied and how much each villager must pay—these are matters also decided by the committee. The committee also deals with administrative disputes between individuals or between an individual and an institution.

If a villager falls on hard times for any reason, perhaps because his crops fail or his fields are flooded, the committee will often reduce his taxes a little and not charge him interest on the money he owes even though the committee itself has to pay interest on any money it borrows. But the committee's discretion in these cases is limited, and if anybody wants further concessions he must go before an arbitration commission which conducts a kind of means test before coming to a decision. The decisions of the arbitration commission are binding. Sometimes the committee submits a matter of this kind to the general council of the village for a decision.

The village has invested the committee with full powers to enforce its rulings and it can do so in various ways: by cutting off water for irrigation, by refusing to accept produce for marketing, by not allowing children to attend school, by withdrawing transport facilities and so on. Not allowing children to attend school is a measure only resorted to when all else has failed and there is no alternative. Fortunately, cases of non-compliance with decisions of the committee are almost non-existent and only very rarely has it had to use its powers of compulsion at all. In fact, during the entire 25 years of Nahalal's existence only three or four villagers have ever had measures of the kind mentioned above taken against them.

The committee, its sub-committees and the members of the

administration come under close scrutiny by the village at its annual general meeting. Every member over eighteen is entitled to ask questions, express opinions, suggest changes and voice criticism on any social or economic matter in the life of the village. The annual general meeting is an important event in the village, because on the decisions taken at the meeting depend all the aspects of village life.

In addition to the annual general meeting, other meetings to discuss various matters are also held at fairly frequent intervals, though not as frequently as in the old days when everything had to be set up from scratch. Nowadays they do not last long either, and often nobody knows at the end of them what Nahalal thinks about the subject under discussion.

The annual general meeting is also the occasion for elections to positions in the various village institutions. Voting is by secret ballot, and 'one member, one job' is the rule. Of course, there are people who offer themselves for election year after year and are never elected, and others who are elected every time. Public affairs cannot be conducted by just anyone. The best men for the job must be chosen. The range of candidates must be widened also so that more people will be trained for public work, especially the younger generation.

At Nahalal we have achieved our aspiration—to be workers and farmers and not have to be concerned with business and trade. Two organisations have been set up—the consumers' supply store, which buys for the villager and his family everything they need apart from clothes and some building materials, and 'Anava' which sells all that he and his family produce.

Anava is divided into three main sections: dairy products; poultry, eggs, fruit and vegetables; grain and seeds. The grain and seed department also supplies fodder and so on for the village work animals, and seed. Anava runs all the village transport, both passenger and goods, runs the water works, a flour mill and a cattle breeding station, and has affiliated with it credit and insurance organisations.

A committee of five elected at the annual general meeting supervise Anava's operations. The annual report is always submitted at the village general meeting and is as exhaustively discussed as any other matter.

The question of woman's place in the social order has always ranked high in the moshav movement. In the early days of Nahalal, some of the women members ran farms of their own and had equal rights with the rest of the members. They proved, over the years, that under moshav conditions they could be householders in the widest possible meaning of the term. Today a woman organises her own life in the moshav, and arranges her daily work to suit her own needs. And her daily work is not restricted to cooking, housework and looking after the children. She also works in the garden or vegetable patch, and in the cowshed.

The independence that women have always enjoyed at Nahalal has revealed their inner strength. They have become real farm women and have proved their ability. Almost every job is open to them. The village poultry farming activities are almost entirely run by women, and they have equal standing with the men in every other kind of work except the very heaviest agricultural labour.

A new generation has grown up at Nahalal, healthy in mind and body, reared on good food and clean surroundings, with flower-filled gardens round their houses and a sympathetic family spirit in their homes. And in all this, the women's handiwork can be seen. For, in the moshav, women have found their rightful place. They have equal rights with the men, and play their full part in all aspects of moshav life.

If a woman is unfortunate enough to be widowed at Nahalal, her farm is not handed over to another family. Instead, a paid farm worker is engaged at the public expense. He does all the heavy physical labour while the woman supervises the running of the house and of the farm. She is also helped to educate her children, so that when they grow up they can take their father's place.

Nahalal was founded with the aim of building a society where there could be no class war. Everyone would be a worker in his own right, living by his own work. There would be no exploiters and no exploited. We have succeeded in our aim and created a new society, a creative, productive society living directly from the land and the work of its hands.

Our economy has been built on the family and its work, and we have employed paid labour only in very exceptional circumstances. Our children have done most of the work and created the village and everything in it. We ourselves worked too hard, for we had to start from nothing. There were not enough hours in the day for us, and we worked on in darkness after the sun had set. We did not do this for material gain, but because we wanted to build here a sound farm economy for the generations which were to come after us. We hope that the next generation will have an easier time. We, however, have a double task to fulfil—to build up Nahalal for the future, and to gain our daily bread from its soil now. This is too much for ordinary mortals to do. And we are constantly anxious for the peace of our society. We do not believe in ourselves, for there have been failures in our working society. A dozen times a day we ask ourselves: 'Have we really created a new society, a juster society?'

One of our fundamental principles when we founded the moshav was that there should be no private ownership of the land. We did not regard other private property with favour either.

We were sure that the limitations we had set ourselves, of living by our own work, would be enough to prevent us amassing goods and property beyond what we needed in order to live, renew our equipment and supplies, and pay the heavy taxes levied upon us.

But as time went by we realised that we had indeed amassed a great deal of property. The value of our land had increased enormously, far exceeding the money originally invested in it. Individual members had saved money. When a member was given a loan or other assistance by one of the settlement institutions like the Keren Hayesod, for example, he had to sign a contract which contained clauses requiring him to obtain the Keren Hayesod's consent before he could transfer his farm to anyone else.

Now, however, when the members of the moshav are no longer bound by such contracts, quite a number of them will wish to sell their farms. If they do, they will put themselves first and sell to the highest bidder, who may well be somebody we would not have chosen to become a member of Nahalal. It would need only a few cases like that to change the character of the village completely and to destroy all the values we have laboured so hard and long to create. The only way to avoid this is for the village to sign a collective contract with the Jewish National Fund, making it impossible for any member to dispose of his land without the

H

consent of the whole village. For even if individuals may default, an entire community will not turn aside from its chosen way of life, but will guard and defend it.

When we founded the village, we knew that we should also need our own professional people and skilled workers. We decided that they would be members but would have smaller plots of land than the rest of us, as their jobs would not permit them to spend much time on farm work.

We had a doctor, a mechanic, a carpenter, book-keepers, and so on. Each was given five dunams of land. This would be enough for a vegetable garden, and some trees and vines which would supply enough fruit for household needs. It would also enable them to grow enough feedingstuff for one cow. While the man worked at his job his family would tend the land, with the man lending a hand for an hour before he went off to his job and another hour at the end of the day. In this way, we thought, the whole family would still be bound up with the land and could participate in village life.

During the first few years our income was very low. We worked very hard indeed and barely made a living. The professional men complained and said that they wanted to be paid at Histadrut rates. They said that their small plots of land merely cost them money, and were no help at all as far as income was concerned. They could not cultivate them properly, and every time they hired a horse or bought a cart they spent more than the things they had bought brought in. They could only work on their land to the detriment of their jobs, and their wives had too much to do to look after it properly. Furthermore, they said they did not agree to being paid the average wage of an agricultural worker. They were skilled men and they wanted to be paid accordingly.

The other members said that the skilled workers had a much better life than they did. The skilled workers had an eight hour day, while everyone else worked far longer hours. Their wives only worked in the house, just as if they lived in the city. City wages would be unfair, especially as their living accommodation was free. In any case, as agricultural workers they could not afford to pay skilled workers such high wages.

There were many bitter discussions on the subject, and the village began to split into two factions. But then the problem was solved. Teachers and doctors and their assistants received their wages from central institutions and no longer needed to be paid by the village. Skilled tradesmen—mechanics, cobblers, blacksmiths, worked for themselves and charged for the work they did. The few remaining people who worked in the various village enterprises were paid at Histadrut rates.

Time has solved all these problems. The professional men and tradesmen and their families have put down roots. Many of their sons and daughters live and work in the village where they were born. There is mutual respect between the two classes, farmers and professionals. Although the latter do not play much part in the public life of the village, in every other respect they are exactly like the farmers.

Ten years after we had first settled at Nahalal, a dreadful thing happened. One evening a bullet shattered the window of a house at Kfar Yehezkiel, wounding a man in the leg. A few months later there was a similar occurrence at Balfouria, and this time somebody was killed. Shortly after that the watchmen of Kfar Hassidim were attacked at night. A few months passed and then a cartload of boys and girls from Yagur was fired on and two people killed.

We were used to sudden attacks and robberies, but whoever had done these things was out to kill. Moreover the fact that all these incidents had happened in the Emek, the very heart of Jewish settlement, proved that the perpetrators had political motives. For more than two years the Government sent police and detectives to try and track down the killers, but without any result.

But in any case, the murderers did not achieve their objective. Settlement and building continued apace. More people came to the Emek and new settlements grew up.

One evening, after a hard day's work in the fields sowing our crops, we had gathered in the communal hall for a meeting. Suddenly there was a loud explosion from somewhere outside, and then we heard screams. We rushed out of the hall and over to Yosef Jacobi's hut where the screams were coming from. When we got there we found the walls and floor and everything in the room spattered with blood. Jacobi's face was covered with blood too, and one hand was almost severed from his arm, hanging by a tendon. Standing there in his smoke-filled hut, his eyes starting from his head and his hair in wild disorder, he asked us if his son was all right. His small son David, aged eight, had escaped our attention for the moment. His face was contorted with agony and he was crying for help.

The ambulance came with a doctor and a nurse, and they took Jacobi and his son away. For the next couple of days we went about wondering whether they would come back to us. They did come back, but they were dead. David's body lay in state in his classroom and the children took it in turns to stay by his body in pairs until midnight. Then the older children took over. Jacobi's body lay in the communal hall.

The whole village went to the funeral. The boy and his father were buried near the other two burial grounds, the Arab and the German. The boy's mother—he was her only child—filled in his grave. She was so brave that day. She did not weep. She did not even shed one tear. Courage like that frightens one.

Five accused faced the court in Haifa. There were two ringleaders, one of whom had confessed to committing murder. They were both poor Arabs, one a peasant and one an artisan from the town. All five had beards which they were growing in a special way, the sign of the group they belonged to. They were wearing little round skull caps, their faces were deadly serious and they muttered prayers the whole time.

They belonged to a terrorist secret society, whose members were all religious Moslems, organised by their priests. They used to manufacture home-made bombs and distribute them among their members in the Arab villages. The society's sole aim was killing, killing the Jews who lived in the settlements scattered over the Emek.

Three hours' walk from Nahalal, in the Nazareth mountains, was the religious Moslem village of Tsipori with several thousand inhabitants. The police discovered that the society had members among them, and knew who they were. They raided the house of Mustafa, the quiet peasant who had carried out his mission successfully. His wife had hidden his revolver and his grenade under her clothes, but when she went to throw them on to the manure heap she was caught by a waiting policeman.

Mustafa stated that he had been incited by a priest. Giloni the artisan, his colleague in the organisation, came to his house at Tsipori on the evening of the murder and they went and prayed. After that they set out for Nahalal, Mustafa armed with a home-made bomb, and Giloni with a rifle. They made their way silently in the darkness to a certain leafy tree in the fields just over a mile from Nahalal. There they sat down and rehearsed their tasks. With Mustafa leading the way they headed directly for Nahalal. They came to a fenced-in yard, entered it in the darkness and reached the row of pomegranate trees planted along the side wall of Yosef Jacobi's modest little hut. Mustafa crept through the trees, opened the shutter, smashed the window-pane and threw his bomb into the hut. Then he and Giloni made off the same way they had come.

Mustafa was hanged, and Giloni, who was recommended for mercy, received fifteen years' hard labour.

At the end of the year we erected a tombstone. Its inscription read:

'While snatching a few moments of rest from his labours, the father was murdered and the son was cut off in the morning of his life while still a child, and before he knew much of life. Their memories are sacred, since they sacrificed themselves for the nation.'

As fate would have it, the disturbances which began in 1935 and lasted uninterruptedly for four years claimed a member of Nahalal as their first victim. The Arabs were well organised, they were armed, and they started by murdering Jews. Then they extended their operations to include Government employees. They mined paths and roads, threw grenades, burnt down plantations, robbed lonely travellers, killed and plundered. At first the Jews did not realise the extent of these Arab activities, and thought that the Government would take energetic steps to stamp them out. It soon became evident, however, that English officialdom was unable or unwilling to prevent Arab attacks and the Jews had to defend themselves. They limited themselves to defence only, and it was their policy never to attack the enemy. Every entrance to the village as well as every exit was blocked with logs and iron bars, wire ropes and agricultural implements.

Sentries were posted, both on foot and mounted, and vehicles circled the village day and night, without a break. All the men in the village, as well as the young women, were trained in the use of weapons. At night the men all slept at various central posts without undressing. Sentries guarded the village during working hours when the rest of the men were in the fields.

The papers were full of stories of murders, burning crops and destroyed plantations. The young people of the village bore the brunt of the disturbances. They kept watch on our Arab neighbours from among the trees and rocks near their villages, listened to their conversations, learnt their signals and met the first onslaught every time there was an attack. The more skilled and experienced youth helped Charles Orde Wingate to guard the oil pipeline, and took part in punitive operations against some of the Arab villages responsible for the disturbances. Some of these young men served as guides for the English in some of their expeditions against Arab villages, and others became policemen and auxilaries, using every possible means of obtaining arms.

By day we worked and by night we guarded our homes. We supplied the Jewish cities and towns with the produce they had previously obtained from the Arabs, and helped them stave off the famine that threatened as the disturbances grew; in 1939 the wave of disturbances hit us directly.

CHAPTER FOUR

MOSHE DAYAN IMPRISONED

Between the years 1922 and 1948 Israel was under British man-datory rule. This not being a political survey of an era but a personal account of a long fruitful period, the writer does not judge or estimate British rule in its different manifestations.

In 1939 the writer's son Moshe (later Commander-in-Chief of the Israeli army) was jailed with a group of 42 boys. They were caught training, were all members of a Hagana course and carried arms—all things prohibited by the British. This chapter deals with the prison period. The whole country was involved—trials, pleas, pride and sorrow—the writer taking part in the struggle both as a father and as a public figure.

He became involved in the political scene, and his range of activities spread beyond the village borders. Here again, the frontier between fatherly feeling and patriotism, between love of a son and hurt pride in a nation, is indistinct. It has been so all through his life. Much of this chapter is taken directly from his diaries of that time.

5th October, 1939. Kalman of Beit Shearim, a neighbouring settle-ment, drove up to the house and informed me with a polite smile that he and his neighbours had seen Moshe my son and some of the other boys who had been arrested, being taken to Acre. They had been caught carrying arms. Someone at Beit Shearim had picked up a note Moshe had managed to throw down, and it was passed on to Ruth. 'Do not worry', it said soothingly. But was *he* unworried?

Kalman came with me to see Ruth, Moshe's wife, and gave her the same details, but neither his smile nor Moshe's note soothed me. It was as if a heavy stone weighed on my heart. I did not see the note. That same evening I had telephoned settlements and individuals and told them that the course at Yavniel would have to be transferred elsewhere. Two British officers had been investigating the young men's activities which were indeed illegal, intending to arrest them, apparently; but they had not been able to find out anything and had left. This was a pretty clear indication that they would return next day in force, surrounding the settlement and imposing a curfew.

The young men attending the course left in two groups, one by bus and one on foot. The second group was late and could not reach their objective, Moledet, while it was still dark. When dawn broke they were still an hour away from Moledet, close to a British Army divisional camp. Arab police and their officers spotted the armed group and arrested them. Moshe and Sukenik were acting as guides for the group and were some 400 yards ahead of them. Moshe was unarmed and Sukenik had a revolver for which he had a licence. The police let the two of them go by into a deep wadi. Then when the main group had been caught, the police chased after Moshe and Sukenik and caught them. The entire group of 43 young men were arrested and taken to Acre.

6th to 8th October. They say that there has been a mistake and they will soon be released. But we are anxious and worried. It is no good sitting at home. We must go to the centre of political life—Jerusalem and the Jewish Agency.

13th October. I have been a frequent visitor at the Agency. I have turned to Ben-Gurion for help and he has assured me that everything is being done that can be done. They cabled the details to Moshe Shertok in London but there was no certainty that the message had arrived or been understood, because they were using an unaccustomed code. However, later on a reply was received from London and it was clear that the message had been understood. They wanted to assure me that if Moshe Shertok knew all about it he would do everything possible. The military authorities had had the assistance of these boys in the past. They had fought side by side with British officers in the Special Night Squads, and Shertok knew about the weapons and the need to defend our settlements. The British officers and men knew that the Hagana always exercised restraint and only used their weapons for self-defence. Wingate, the British officer who had collaborated with them, was in London. He knew Moshe personally and would help. Dr. Chaim Weizmann was also there, and the two of them would work together for the boys' release. That was what I wanted to believe, anyhow.

Saturday. The first visit to the fortress prison at Acre. We went together by special bus from Haifa, but not everybody knew about the visit so there were not many of us. We were at the prison gate by nine o'clock, and exactly on time we were allowed inside. Our names were taken, and each prisoner was allowed two visitors. We saw them on the roof some way away, waiting for us. After an hour they were marched in in two tight ranks, accompanied by warders. They looked over towards us, laughing and cheerful. Moshe, deeply tanned, smiled at me but I detected worry and sadness in his smile. They were put behind a wire screen, a few yards from where we were standing. When we spoke to each other we had to shout to make ourselves heard because of the noise, and also because where the boys were, behind the screen, was lower than the spot we were standing on. . . Police and detectives were present, so there was no chance of giving the prisoners any really interesting news.

We had to tell them something though. We told them that everything was being done to try and help them. We asked how they had been caught and what had happened to their weapons. Moshe told me that he had been unarmed. They had been thoroughly searched in the prison, and some of them had been beaten (though not badly), but came through all right. Moshe asked about the farm—how far advanced sowing was and whether the fields had been prepared. Our boys, proud, independent, jealous of their freedom of action, were in prison guarded by Arab policemen.

After ten minutes the visit ended and we were conducted out of the fortress with tears in our eyes, leaving our loved ones there in the tyranny of prison.

The high walls of the fortress were of stone, and they were thick with a deep moat all round and watch towers at the corners, manned by police with machine-guns and searchlights. Police were on duty at the gate and inside the prison yard and accompanied every prisoner wherever he went and whatever he did.

I passed through Acre without seeing it. I could not see anything. One thought possessed my mind: 'Moshe, my son, is in prison. I must set him free, he committed no crime, but I cannot'.

Then we began to receive intermittent letters from Moshe.

Acre, 17th October. 'They take their time delivering letters, and I do not think that this will reach you before Saturday. Even if one of you comes to visit me, it will be impossible for us to speak to to each other or to hear what the other is saying.

'At the moment life here is easy compared with the life of convicted prisoners. It has not rained yet and our cell is dry, though very dirty. The attitude of the police is not bad and the food is good.

'It is impossible to say anything about prison life and our letters have to be short. One thing is clear to me: happy is he who has not come to this. It is not the conditions which are depressing but the inactivity, the certain knowledge that one can do nothing except obey the orders of the Arab warder and carry them out immediately.

'Just the same, by comparison with the hundreds of convicts here (many of them sentenced to 10 or 15 years' hard labour), we feel that we are all right. This is especially so because we are not criminals, and all 43 of us are together. That is the only way to keep our morale up—to compare our situation with that of the rest of the inmates here. We have met many Arabs here who have had skirmishes with the night squads in the past. Some have had limbs amputated, some are blind and some creep about on all fours because of injuries to their spinal cords.'

20th October. Ruth, my daughter-in-law, has gone to stay with her parents in Jerusalem for a while with little Yael. It is much better for her to be with her mother and father than on her own. Little Yael tried to walk and made talking noises. It is heartbreaking to think of her being separated from her father. Why can't Moshe be here with his beloved baby during her first months of life? Why have they taken a father away from his child? Every time Yael tries to say something, or stretches out her arms to embrace me, it breaks my heart. Ruth feels this way too, but restrains herself admirably.

It is clear from conversations I have had with members of the Hagana that the Jewish Agency intends to put forward the argument that the accused men had just been out on their own affairs as private individuals, and just happened to meet each other. Is this the right line to take? There are arguments for and against. If they say: 'This is the independent defence force of the Yishuv and we are responsible for them', what will happen if the authorities demand that we disband and reveal our organisers and leaders? We should be in a difficult position and would have to comply. If on the other hand the 43 are sacrificed, it will be a big sacrifice but at least it will be limited to them. The third choice is to say that we know the 43 and are certain of their good intentions and good behaviour, but that they just combined for the training of their own accord. In that case though, they might receive severe sentences. The authorities want to destroy the Hagana and get their revenge on the Jewish Agency which they hate because it refuses to be humbled. It seems to me that we can expect the judgement to be a hard one. Despite the fact that the Agency says it knows these boys and gives them a good character, it has chosen to reject its responsibility for the 43 in order to preserve the existence of the Hagana intact.

I would have preferred a more aggressive attitude. The leaders of the Jewish Agency and the Hagana should say to the authorities: 'The 43 and ourselves are part of the same organisation—we are responsible for the self-defence of the Yishuv of which we are a part. You must put the entire Hagana on trial, and not just these 43 young men.' There is the danger, however, that they will imprison the Hagana leaders and confiscate our arms. They may also institute proceedings against the Agency. The danger is there all right, but it is possible to overcome it by a proper political operation. Then the Hagana will be recognised as part and parcel of the Yishuv, and account will be taken of its situation vis-à-vis the Arabs, which has been the same throughout our existence in Palestine, particularly during the disturbances. The Agency has chosen not to adopt these tactics, however. It prefers to endanger the 43 rather than put the entire Hagana in jeopardy.

Perhaps the Agency is right, but the conclusion is obvious—the 43 are in serious danger.

The Agency representatives still refuse to try and see the G. O. C. until he sends for them, both for reasons of prestige and because they are not sure of success. The days go by, and although Dr. Joseph had a meeting with the head of the C. I. D. nothing came of it. They have appointed lawyers, and consultations are being held to decide how the defence should be conducted.

In the end the Agency has asked for a meeting with General Barker, but he refused to discuss the matter until after the trial. The attempts to temporise have failed and there will be a trial.

23rd October. According to brief messages from the prison, the boys are being energetically interrogated and some of them have been beaten in order to get them to supply the 'evidence' their interrogators want. Feelings are running high.

At visiting time I asked Moshe about this, even though there were detectives there. He tried to reassure me, but did not deny anything. Generally speaking, he said, the attitude of their gaolers was correct. Our boys are proud and full of courage and show a brave face to the world. I was proud of them, but saddened by them as well. The English second-in-command went past, limping as he walked. He was angry and everybody was frightened of him. The warders grew stern while the convicts busied themselves emptying the dustbins.

The boys were taken back to detention. A last smile and then further conversation was forbidden. It is doubtful whether they will be given the parcels we brought for them. All the grapefruit were given to the Jewish policemen. I do not suppose Moshe will get the walnuts from the leafy tree in the garden, which was planted specially for him. My dear son, how sad your eyes were when you saw 9-month-old Yael, your daughter, through the wire without being able to embrace her or kiss her. I pity you all—Moshe, Ruth and Yael.

Ben-Zion Dinaburg requested a committee meeting, so we all met at Beit Zvi in Jerusalem, and went to see Ben-Gurion at the Jewish Agency. I suggested that I should go to London to assist Dr. Weizmann in his efforts on behalf of the arrested boys, and Dinaburg supported my suggestion. The journey will be dangerous and it is doubtful too whether I am really suitable for a task of that kind, but B-G agreed and instructed the secretariat to obtain the necessary visas for me. They have been refused.

B-G agreed to my going to London, to reassure me, even though he doubted whether my visit would achieve anything. They do not think the sentence will be a severe one. I am less optimistic. In my view London should be the centre of operations. Even though Shertok is there, fully understands the situation and is doing all he can to remedy it, we should still concentrate the rest of our efforts on London and not locally. It is doubtful whether he knows all the details, since it is very difficult to get information through the censorship. I asked Berl Katzenelson what he thought the outcome of the trial would be, but his answer was not very illuminating. I have the impression that the Agency is not telling us what is going on because of the possible danger to the Hagana and its leaders.

27th October. The day of the trial draws near. It is sowing time now, and Aviva and Zorik (our two younger children) are working half-days in the fields lending a hand. I guide the plough while Aviva controls the mules and sows the wheat in Shimron field. I spread fertiliser and she sows seed until midday. Zorik takes over the sowing in the afternoon. While I work, Moshe's face is constantly before my eyes. He wrote recently:

'I am claiming my right to send a weekly letter. We have still not been tried yet. Once the trial is over, if we are found guilty we shall only be allowed one letter or a visit every two months. The trial is due to begin the day after tomorrow and we are a little tense about it. Our lawyers have not been to see us yet to prepare our defence. If the trial is a short one the verdict may be announced before Saturday, and if we are found guilty there will be no visit.

'At the moment we are managing to keep ourselves clean. We shave twice a week and have had our hair cut. We have been promised a shower twice a week, and we certainly need it. The food is good and we are allowed on the roof in the fresh air every day. Conditions are excellent, but the prospect of their remaining unchanged after the end of the trial is not very bright. For all that, we are impatient and do not want the trial to be delayed. I do not know when this letter will arrive, but if there is any doubt about your reply getting here before the trial do not send it, because it might be considered as being my allowance for two months, and you would not be able to visit me. I saw that Dad was very worried. It is not worth worrying or being too anxious, because it does not help.'

25th-29th October. The day of the trial. All the family went to the army camp on the Nahariya road. After Acre, the road curves left towards the sea, and the camp is about one and a quarter miles from there. There was a military guard on the gate, and we stood and waited for the prisoners. It was a long wait. They were handcuffed to each other in threes, and as their transport drove off we tried to find our loved ones and exchange a glance with them. Yes, there was Moshe, manacled to two of his comrades like the rest! The gate was closed in our faces. We walked nervously back and forth for hours an end, not knowing how the trial was going and how the judges would judge our sons. What evil had they done, after all? The lawyers were inside in the yard, and so were Ruth and her father Zvi. They were close to the scene of the trial, while we all waited for news.

At noon they were taken back to the prison, and an hour later brought back again for the trial to continue.

After three days, it had still not ended. The court adjourned for Saturday and Sunday and resumed on Monday. We waited outside the gate.

30th October. On the last day of the trial I managed to get into the court, and sat down not far from the prisoners. Moshe was nervous and did not want to speak one word to me. A British policeman stood next to him watching his every move. Moshe knows English well and gave evidence with courage and honesty. He said that the Government knew that the Jews must defend themselves and that this harmed nobody. Moshe Dayan, 24 years old, born in Degania, brought up at Nahalal, my son!

The prosecutor's speech shocked us. He likened them to a band of murderers. Then we told ourselves that we ought not to attach too much importance to this, because it was his job to make a speech of that kind. Dr. Eliash made an impassioned speech for the defence. He described the tragedy of the Jews and explained that it was only right for a young Jew to give of his strength in the fight against Hitler, the destroyer of Jewry. His words brought tears to our eyes.

The court adjourned for ten minutes. We could feel the mounting tension as everyone waited. Then their names were called, and they stood up smartly, one by one, with straight backs, sons of a free motherland. Then the sentences were announced. 42 of them received ten years, and the forty-third fifteen years.

We sat there as if thunderstruck, not grasping the full meaning of what we had heard. Ruth began weeping. Moshe gritted his teeth. The boys were handcuffed again and quickly marched out to the waiting transport. 'Don't lose heart, Moshe. We'll get the sentence quashed!' I shouted as he passed me.

Moshe did not say a word. His heart was heavy within him and refused to be comforted. I took my time walking back to the gate, where I would have to break the news to the family. I waited by the lorry and looked at the faces of the condemned boys. I did not take my eyes off Moshe, as if I wanted to make up for the years that he would be away from my sight.

Suddenly one of the boys shouted: 'The glory of Israel shall not be betrayed!' The words trembled in the air, and brought tears to my eyes.

The boys, manacled were taken back to the prison. We returned to Haifa by bus, every one of us weeping unashamedly at the fate that had befallen our dear ones.

1st November. Will it really happen? Ten years! They have been sentenced as if they were murderers! For four years these boys turned night into day, fighting gangs of Arab murderers who were attacking the British Army and the Jews. They put their lives in danger every hour of the day and night. After this cooperation between the Army and the Jews, the British have turned on us and accused us of being criminals. This is betrayal!

The family have gone home and I am on the way to Jerusalem from Tel Aviv, where the sentences have already been announced. At the Executive Committee meeting I asked that the party's political committee should convene. Sprinzak encouraged me to travel to Jerusalem and promised to call the meeting for the next day. In the morning Sprinzak and B. Katzenelson met Ben-Gurion in his room, and after discussing the matter for an hour or so they authorised him to go to London. They also discussed whether he ought to try and obtain an interview with the G.O.C., who would have to confirm the findings of the court.

The political committee meeting did not last long. B-G asked the committee to express their concern at the harsh measures introduced by the Government, which had that week announced that permission would no longer be given to Jews to enter the country, and that only a limited number of non-Jews would be allowed to do so. The committee's protest against the travesty of justice that the trial represented was not as powerful as the one that had already been made. Even before the meeting started Ben-Gurion said to me: 'It will not be a catastrophe even if these boys are imprisoned for a few years.' This infuriated me, because I could certainly not get used to the idea. The members of the committee commiserated with me, and Sprinzak's sincere help sustained me at this difficult time.

3rd November. I have been under pressure from the Council of Settlements and the Agricultural Centre itself to take up a position there. But I do not want to work at the Centre, and in any case I cannot consider taking on any public work at this time. I explained my situation at the meeting and asked that the matter should be deferred.

10th November. B-G had a meeting with the G.O.C. in the name of the Agency Executive, and asked for the sentences to be reduced. The content of the talks was not revealed.

12th November. The news that the boys now have to wear prison garb, have had their hair cropped and have been confined inside the fortress has depressed me unutterably. They sleep on mats on the stone floor with two army blankets each. They have two meals a day—pitta (Arab bread) and a few olives; and pitta with a sort of porridge made from vegetables cooked in rancid oil, which it is impossible to eat. The boys are hungry. All they wear on their feet is sandals, because they are not allowed to wear socks, or have them brought in from outside. Nothing whatever, food or anything else, can be sent in to them. Two or three of them have already fallen ill and are running a high temperature. The Arab doctor is more like a butcher than a doctor. Dov Hos, representing the Histadrut (Workers' Federation) has had a meeting with the G.O.C. He explained the Yishuv's position during the disturbances and pointed out how little the Army had been able to do on occasions of that kind. The Yishuv cannot give up its arms to the authorities, for difficult times are

likely to recur and we cannot rely on the Army for our safety The
G.O.C. had been hostile at the beginning of the interview, but
he had softened by the end of it and said that he would consider
the matter carefully before confirming the sentences.

18th November. The day when the sentences will be confirmed
is slowly approaching. The political committee has decided
that no newspapers will appear on that day and that there will be a
general strike. I am writing a letter to the G.O.C., though I
do not believe he will pay any attention to it.

'I, an ordinary countryman, am writing this letter, although
the prospects of any attention being paid to it are slim indeed.
What I write comes from deep within my heart. I am taking
the liberty of writing to the Military Governor of Palestine in
time of war, because I think that it is possible to appeal to his
conscience. In the name of conscience, I call on you to stop.
You now have completely in your power 43 young men who are
the bearers of a historic promise of deep meaning for their people.
This promise is to rebuild the ruins of Palestine, so that it may
be a refuge for our persecuted people, where they can start a new
national life.

'These young men were born and brought up in the days of
the Balfour Declaration, and even while they were still children
they nourished the hope that the English would help us to build
our national home. They were brought up in a movement which
aims at building the land through work, and they have made the
idea of working and building a reality. They have been brought
up to have friendly relations with our Arab neighbours. They
have also been brought up to recognise the unpleasant necessity
for self-defence.

'Their fathers, emigrants from Russia, Poland and Rumania,
learnt from the savagery unleashed on them in their countries
of origin. They trained themselves and their children to bear
arms in their own defence. From the very beginning of Jewish
settlement in Palestine we have had to suffer sudden attacks on
our settlements, as well as on people in the cities, the villages,
the fields and on the roads, by Arabs intent on robbing and
plundering and murdering for the sake of murdering. Savagery
and horror have been our lot during the years of the British
Mandate. All this has compelled us to build up our own defence.

I

Jews have not attacked Arab villages or individuals anywhere in any way, except in a very few isolated instances.'

I had a letter from Moshe, trying to set my mind at rest:

'It is obvious that you are worrying unduly, because conditions here continue to be very good. There is certainly no reason for you to go abroad. Everything that could be done has been done, and now we must await the outcome. After that we must wait for a general amnesty, if there is going to be one. Until then we have to make arrangements and deal with various matters. It is a pity that we counted on receiving light sentences.

'For some reason the question of the books is still unsettled. If it is a matter of money, every one of us will ask his family for the book he needs in order to continue his studies. We are well organised here and ready for anything (as if there is any alternative!).

'Generally speaking, life here is interesting (particularly if one only looks on), and we celebrated the three days of Ramadan and enjoyed them. Our relations with the Arabs here are very good.

'Write and tell me if anything important has happened in the Yishuv. I wrote a letter of thanks today to Wingate, the one and only decent Englishman. Remember me to Aviva and Kishek (his pet name for Zohar, his brother).'

Sitting in a restaurant in Jerusalem with Berl and Sprinzak, I told them about the British soldiers in one of the camps who said that the 43 must have been in contact with the Germans because they had been found with German and Polish weapons. One of the soldiers said that he would have stood our boys against the wall and shot them. What crazy notions they have about us!

I said that we ought to publish a pamphlet explaining who the 43 were and why they had been imprisoned. Such a pamphlet should be produced in several languages, especially English, for the British Army in Palestine, and for everyone who did not know what the whole affair was about. Devora had first mentioned the idea at home, because she remembered a similar pamphlet in Russian which had appeared in the 1880's, explaining the aims of the Socialist party.

27th November. Morning in Haifa. The Hebrew newspapers have not appeared as a protest against the sentences. The Yishuv is on strike from 10 a.m. till noon, and in the evening places of amusement will be closed. The *Palestine Post* has appeared. 42 of the boys have had their sentences reduced from 10 years to 5. The other one has got 10 years instead of life. *Hamashkif*, the Revisionist paper, has been the only Hebrew paper to appear, proving that it is completely out of touch with public opinion.

I went to Tel Aviv with Devora. The organisers of the strike stopped the bus at Hadera at 10 o'clock. Tens of buses were stopped on the road for two hours. Arab and British military vehicles passed by and their occupants asked what the strike was about. They were impressed when we told them. Official leaflets issued by the Va'ad Leumi and the Tel Aviv Municipality, explaining the reason for the strike, had been distributed in the streets, and many illegal pamphlets have been circulating as well. Their theme is the same: 'We have all been brought to trial and we have all been sentenced.'

28th November. At my suggestion a cable was sent to Mr. Green, the American labour leader, requesting him to make representations to the British Labour Party on behalf of the 43.

29th November. Our main preoccupation now is to get better conditions in the prison for our boys. The Agency is unwilling to take any action, because if it does this may be construed as meaning that the Agency acquiesces in the sentences. Or perhaps because it does not want to ask for special conditions and have the request turned down. The only thing to do is to use indirect methods. By establishing cautious contact with police and warders at the prison we have managed to make a few small loopholes. Letters have been smuggled in to the prisoners. If this were discovered it would endanger their position, but it had to be done.

10th December. Moshe told us from prison that they joined in the Yishuv's strike. For 24 hours the prisoners did not accept any food, and they told the prison governor that they were striking against the injustice of their sentences. Moshe's letters are our only consolation. After the strike he wrote:

'Well we have come through the second stage all right, and now we have to wait for a reduction in our sentences. The strike throughout the country gave us great satisfaction, and we also declared a 24-hour hunger strike in protest against our sentences.

'I know how difficult the position always is on the farm, and this year it looks as if it will be particularly so. I know also how worried you are because of me and what has happened is playing on your nerves— too much so. You seem to think that being in prison here is like the descriptions in Dostoievsky and Wassermann or as it used to be in Turkish times, but it is not. Certainly our room is not particularly beautiful or luxurious, but up to now, at any rate, our food and clothing have been satisfactory, everything is reasonably clean, and we are not badly treated. We have even managed to get rid of the lice (everything here is very well disinfected). We have been given decent bedding, another blanket, etc.

'The next question is work. We must see that we get good jobs here. I do not think that it will be worth trying to have us distributed among the various prisons, now that we are so well organised.

'Everyone helps and learns from everyone else (some of the prisoners are still only children). Remember, again, that we are by no means sunk in the depths of depression. On the contrary, we are in good spirits, study a lot, spend most of the daylight hours in the open, eat well, and sleep well at night. Everything is perfectly clean here. What encourages us most and what we wait for more than anything else are letters, so please write and tell us about everything, if possible on this airmail paper.'

I replied:

'My son, I was happy when I read of your proud attitude, and your participation in the Yishuv's strike. Your political maturity in internal matters, the fact that you have dissociated yourselves from the Revisionists, and that you told the prison authorities that the strike was in protest against your sentences, all gladdened my heart. Just the same, be careful. There is a war on, and the authorities are quite ruthless. The Yishuv behaved very well. All places of entertainment were closed in the evening, the Executive Committee and Tel Aviv Municipality distributed pamphlets and leaflets, and *Bematzor* the illegal broadsheet. I am telling you all this in case news of it has not reached you yet.

'D. Ben-Gurion, in his survey of the situation, said that there are two opposing forces in the Government, one friendly to us, one hostile. The G.O.C. is directly responsible to the Secretary for War (Hore-Belisha) and the fact that H-B is a Jew does not make him inclined to defend the Jews. On the other hand the Chief of the General Staff is very friendly towards us and is sending cables requesting that the sentences should be quashed or reduced. The Chief of Staff promised Dr. Weizmann that the entire case will be reviewed again in six months' time... Let us hope that the tide will turn in our favour, because your fate depends on it. They are considering our participation on the western front. Important personalities consider that we must participate, for on this will depend our future once the War is over and national frontiers come to be redrawn. The War will spread to the east soon, and we must prepare for it.

'Your conditions have improved, and everything possible is being done outside to improve them still further. We must be patient now. As far as being split up is concerned, at the moment it is impossible to decide what would be in your best interests. Time will tell. Dov went to see the head warders, but I do not know what transpired. Ruth has not yet decided whether to return to Nahalal or stay in Jerusalem. Mother and I spent a day in Jerusalem with the family and stayed the night. We were delighted to be able to see Yael. She is wonderful, so quiet and yet so alert and bursting with health. She is coming along nicely, so lovable and good.

Yours,
Dad.'

The changed conditions were reflected in Moshe's letters:

'.... It has been raining here for the last few days. Is it raining at home as well? The food and supply situation generally has become very bad here lately. We have still not received the first consignment of socks we were sent. Still, despite that, things are not too bad. I hope D.H. (Dov Hos) has decided to try to do something about getting us transferred from here. We all want to get away from here, because if we start travelling about a bit we might get home in the end.'

'In the last few days the attitude of the authorities has grown much stricter. We have not even been allowed to see a newspaper, so you will have to resume sending me your surveys of the situation outside. I am writing to you in the dark, and my mood is none

123

too cheerful, even though it is Chanuka now and after many requests we have managed to get some candles. It is completely dark now. . . .'

And again:

'D.H. was here today. We gave him the details of our life here and he promised to see what he could do to help us. We are working in the open. I am in the garden and am very happy with the work and the conditions, but it is a pity that one develops such an appetite. In the course of his work one of us sees the newspapers, so we feel a bit more in touch with the world outside. In future you will not need to send us your general surveys, but please do tell us what is happening behind the scenes. Zorik and Aviva have written about Nahalal and the farm. I have heard that Mother has written a highly successful and moving feuilleton about us and that it has appeared in *Bematzor*. Please send it to us. We have also heard about B. Katzenelson's message. In my opinion it was not right only to mention two of us, but just the same please convey our regards and thanks to him. What about the rains, and the crops, and the financial position? What are the prospects of having Jewish units in the British Army?'

Two days later:

'See that they send us text-books, particularly for English and Arabic, and also the Hebrew classics (Bialik, the Aggada, the Bible with commentaries). We are all working at easy jobs, most of us in the open air. I am working in the small garden, a good place to work, except that it is walled in and one cannot see anyone or anything. The Governor has said that soon some of us will be transferred from Acre. Dad, write and tell me what else the Agency, Va'ad Leumi and other institutions intend to do about our sentences. It seems to me that nothing can be done until June, so we can stay here peacefully for a year. If we remain at Acre, and if conditions do not worsen, things will not be so bad. The food is adequate, the work is good and we have the chance of studying. Of course it is no special pleasure to acquire an education at Acre, but it is not a disaster. Morale is high and relations between us are good. Please make every effort to write about everything (on thin paper)—how many litres of milk each cow gives, and how the crops are coming along. You write and tell me about everything that has been happening on the farm and at home and about what the youngsters are doing, and I'll write to you about everything that is happening here.'

He wrote to his sister as well:

'Aviva, we received candles for Chanuka, the feast of lights, so we can write an hour longer in the evenings. It is a serious business and must be carried out in secret. Anyone who is caught gets solitary confinement and is put on pitta and water. This means losing our "hummus" and halva rations, and they are the sort of rations we don't like losing. Tell Zorik that I shall be writing to him in a few days in detail about what is happening here. They are going to hang a prisoner who killed another prisoner during the night with a hammer, because the murdered man had insulted him the evening before.'

Moshe wrote to his brother Zorik:

'I promised to tell you about my life in prison, and now I am writing to tell you just a little about it. When they bring a man here under arrest he wears his own clothes until his trial. He does not do any work and can have food brought in from outside. They treat the people under arrest (Arabs) very badly indeed, because they are not "respectable" citizens. They just get a mat to sleep on and two blankets. They are given only half-portions of food—"that's enough for anyone under arrest", is what the policemen say. If there is not enough accommodation for them all they sleep in the shower room. All this is apart from the blows they receive because they are not familiar with the law.

'Prisoners are put into categories according to the length of their sentence. Those sentenced to be hanged are dressed in purple and kept in the cells the whole time. They are given any food they want (on condition that it doesn't cost more than ten piastres a day, of course). Most of them go to the gallows silent and unafraid, although their families weep heart-rendingly when they come to visit them for the last time. Prisoners with life sentences are dressed in brown and wear black caps. They work in the yard and are the best treated of all. Most of them are educated men who used to belong to Arab gangs, and our relations with them are excellent. Their leaders are El Kassem's men. One of them, who has been to America and is an American national, enjoys "special treatment." Some other time I'll explain this to you.

'Short-term prisoners, those sentenced to three months and

so on, are allowed to work in the yard, but they are the most despised category of all and have to clean out the latrines. When a policeman goes up to a prisoner his first question to him is "How long are you in for?" If the prisoner answers "three months" he gets a box on the ear that makes his head swim and is sent to clean down the stairs. This task is carried out as follows: There are eight men with floorcloths, in two groups of four and they are supposed to wash down the stairs. But in fact only the second four do any washing down, because the warder in charge stands over them the whole time. The others do not even wet their floorcloths, let alone bend down to wash the floor, and they are being hit all the time.

'Any prisoner who has tried to escape is given a red uniform so that it will be easy to keep an eye on him in future. He has to work inside, and his sentence is increased.

'Every prisoner who is not ill has to work, and every day 700 of us go out to our various jobs here—kitchen work, laundry work, cleaning out the latrines, disinfecting, working in the Jewish kitchen, the carpenter's shop or the cobbler's shop, making mail bags, tailoring, pressing, gardening, labouring, hospital work, looking after the mental cases, working in the office, etc. A convict sergeant and a convict corporal are in charge of each group and are responsible for the work. They are usually long-term prisoners. They are promoted to the job after eight or ten years in gaol, and after having greased the requisite palms and informed on convicts breaking prison rules.'

In another letter Moshe wrote:

'Does Zorik take any interest in what I write about the prison? We see the newspapers almost every day, but even so we can feel how prison life is gradually gaining the upper hand over the life we used to lead outside. Our old life is just a memory. Our thoughts revolve around the sandwich we get here and our lives have become dull and miserable. That is why I am looking forward to beginning my studies, especially if we can get a teacher from outside.

28th December. The villagers all came to offer consolations to the 'mourners.' Everybody sympathises with us, and has made our troubles his own. Moshe continues to tell us about his 'new life' and his 'work':

'We have not yet begun our studies. The last few days have been rainy, and today is the first good weather we have had. Have you had rain at home, and was it enough? How are the fields looking and the cattle sheds? What sort of impression did this place make on Aviva? I am sure it was a most unfavourable one. Although Acre prison makes a dreadful impression on a person seeing it for the first time, everything you see is superficial. In fact things are quite well organised, especially at the moment—food, newspapers, letters, clothing, hygiene. The question of visits needs attention however.

'I think of Aviva now and again, and of Zorik and Yael and all the younger generation. Do they realise what dark days they are growing up in? Even here, when we read the newspapers our hearts sink.

'Perhaps you who are outside, children, cannot see things as they really are. Perhaps you cannot realise how events are shaping in Poland, but I can visualise them very well. . . . .

'I think that this is the first time that there have been more than 120 Jewish prisoners at Acre—and they are not criminals. How much hidden suffering there is inside the walls of Acre now. 35 sailors have been imprisoned for aiding illegal immigration. Every day they stand and look out to sea. In the middle stands the captain, with his officers on either side, together with the engine room men, the wireless operator, etc. Most of them are Russians; they swear most artistically, play cards, spit and sing. One of them does beautiful paintings. There are also some English and French negroes in the crew, and the whole lot are here because they tried to help Jews to immigrate into Palestine!

'Some of the prisoners here are lads of 17 or 18, Sephardis from Tiberias and Jerusalem. When the Arabs killed members of their families, these boys did not stand aside with folded arms but fired back with rifles. For this they have been sentenced to life! My friends Ben-Yosef and Hankin are here, and 34 Revisionists, most of them very young. Although I do not hold their party in very high regard, I look on them as belonging with us and representative of Jewish suffering today. And there are boys from Ginossar, who at any other time would have received decorations. Who knows what they will receive now? And of course, we are here too.

'Most of the Arab prisoners here were sentenced for their participation in the disturbances, and so they can be considered to represent the general attitude of Arabs towards Jews today. Every day we all go out for exercise under the supervision of a British officer and sergeant. Personal relations between us, the Revisionists and the Arabs are excellent—in fact I am writing this letter with a pencil borrowed from one of the El Kassem gang, the first one to be gaoled after the murder of Rosenfeld. Most of the gang members are idealists and religious believers, not mercenaries. And personal suffering unites us.

'Just the same, I believe that all this will pass. I shall never forget the visits here of the families of those condemned to hang, but I believe that the hangings will stop and that all death sentences will be commuted to life imprisonment. But in the meantime we must be strong and believe'. (24. 12. 39.)

'All the minor matters have been arranged now, except for the dentist. Somebody ought to find out what conditions are like at Athlit and explore the possibility of our being transferred there. I am waiting for "good news" from Moshe Shertok, although I do not believe that anything more will be done beyond requesting a reduction of our sentences on the 6th of June. We have heard various rumours about big army reinforcements being sent to Palestine. Is this true, and are there signs that the War is coming closer to us here?

'Mother writes that the pain of knowing that we are imprisoned is so great that she cannot write or talk about it. I do not know how to explain to you that the affair is not such a catastrophe, particularly in the special conditions under which we are here. Of course, I am in prison and will certainly have to serve the requisite sentence, but this is not a grievous disaster.

'It is quite simply a prison term which has to be served, and then I shall be released and resume a normal life. The Revisionists here have been accorded the same special treatment as us and we are naturally pleased about this. I would like to know if they will also be included in the request for reduced sentences.' (25.12.39)

'In answer to your question about how prisoners can put on weight, Dad, it is quite simple. Those who can obtain money from outside receive additional food. Did the Arab prisoners here get better food at home? Apart from that, they do hardly any work here. We are all supposed to work but nobody does much, even in the workshops. When the Governor comes in everyone bangs away with his hammer and makes a lot of noise, but that is all.

'I imagine that my prison uniform does not give Dad much pleasure, especially the trousers with a patch on the seat like Arab sailors' trousers. Nonetheless the clothes we have to wear are warm and clean. They are washed once a week and disinfected every fortnight. We have a hot shower once a week.

'Our daily routine is now as follows. We get up at 5.30, fold our blankets and go out on parade. The Arab policeman never knows exactly how many men are present, and relies on our honesty. We go out to work and are given a "sandwich" made from Agency bread, and a piece of chocolate. At 11 o'clock we return to our room and are given a piece of halva or some olives and an orange, "Governor's pitta", and our tea. At 12.30 we go out again until 3 o'clock. Then we come back again and have a meal—lentils, rice, aubergines or something similar—and three times a week we get a piece of meat.

'I work in a walled garden, and it is quite a beautiful one. Nobody bothers me, and the policeman only supervises when the Governor comes round. He warns me when the Governor is approaching and then I bend over the flower beds and work. One of the long-term prisoners, a sergeant, has asked us not to work too hard because if we do there will be no work left for tomorrow. Altogether there are nine of us in the garden, seven Jews and two Arabs, doing work which could be done by one girl in two hours a day'.

30th December. I gave a report on the committee's activities at the village annual meeting. I did not know whether to stand for election to the committee again. In the event, I did not refuse because there were several matters I had started, which I wanted to finish. The principal ones were the eradication of contagious abortion from our herds, the introduction of a village income tax, and the setting up of a mutual benefit society. My work on the committee strengthened my contacts with the village, and this factor alone was enough to impel me to carry on with my public work. The elections were held and I was again elected, and started my second year's work with the committee.

Moshe's letters are not the most reassuring letters one could receive.

He writes:

'In the last few days the attitude towards us has changed for the worse. There have been searches and two of the boys have been put in solitary confinement. If there is any possibility of a transfer from here it should be explored, and quickly. If not, the Jewish policemen here must be better organised. Study facilities have not been arranged yet, either, and because of the bad relations which exist at present we are in no position to press the matter with the Governor.'

Some time later:

'Again you are worrying, and every minor happening here has become something of enormous importance by the time you have finished thinking about it. You must realise that prison is prison and not a hotel, and the inmates cannot always have daily meals. At the moment everything is all right again. We are well, and we sleep and study and eat and hope.

'I believe that we would be allowed to have a teacher from outside if we asked for one.'

3rd February. Saturday. It is a beautiful sunny winter's morning. Ten of us went to Acre in two cars for our first visit since the boys were sentenced, three months ago. Ruth has been waiting all week, and she has been given permission to take little Yael with her to visit Moshe. I can just imagine his excitement at seeing his daughter. She was a year old yesterday and walks and says "Daddy." She is dressed in a long blue winter coat, with white pockets and a white hat and she is full of life and looks wonderful.

There were hundreds of relatives and friends of the 43 at Acre. The previous commandant has been replaced by a new one, and Dov has not yet been able to make advance arrangements for more convenient visiting conditions. The deputy commandant, Grant, supervised the visitors and was not at all friendly or helpful. Only two people could visit each prisoner. Five of us went in, but we were turned back at the yard. Only Ruth and Devora were allowed to see Moshe, and they would not let Ruth take Yael in with her, Ruth cried bitterly, but Grant remained unmoved. Although the law permits ten minutes for a visit, this time it lasted only three or four minutes. Ruth and Devora hardly had time to exchange a word with Moshe. When they came out they said his eyes were red and painful. He seemed apathetic and asked whether there were still searches and arrests after the search at Ben Shemen. He looked fairly well, and his prison number was prominently stamped on his uniform.

Scores of us were turned back and not allowed to visit the prisoners. A woman burst into tears, but the policeman laughed, put her out of the gate and closed and bolted it. A group of us stayed near the fortress and waited for the afternoon, hoping that we might be allowed in then. From one of the prison windows the prisoners were sending morse messages by waving a hand-kerchief tied to a stick. Our 13-year old son Zohar, the only one among us who could understand morse, was reading them and passing them on to us.

After a few minutes an English detective appeared. He was furiously angry, and ordered Zorik to go with him. When Ruth and Devora asked why, he said that he was going to detain Zorik for signalling to prisoners, which was forbidden, particularly in wartime. The boy was taken off to the prison and we followed. The gate was closed in our faces before we had a chance to go in. Looking very serious and a little frightened, though by no means panic-stricken, young Zorik followed the detective, and I called Feitelson who dealt with matters concerning the prisoners. I thought of asking to be allowed to enter the prison to be with the boy, but in the meantime I made a sign to him that he should not answer any questions and should deny that he knew morse. I was very much afraid they would beat him. We walked up and down agitatedly for half an hour until they finally released him. In the afternoon we drove back dejectedly, not speaking to one another.

7th February. Moshe hastened to write to us immediately after the visit:

'Mother must have been depressed when she left here, so I am writing now although there is nothing special to write about. I know that our cropped heads and our prison uniform do not lend us added charm. The Arab and English policemen, partic-ularly the brutal ones among them, do not imbue anyone with confidence. But this is, after all, a prison. It is sometimes possible to obtain special treatment, but external appearances can never be improved. Of course, to know all this is one thing and to actually see it another, and I can understand that it must have been a shock to Mother and to Ruth to catch sight of me suddenly, but what can one do?

'Do not think that prison life has broken me and that I am a dejected prisoner who accepts what is given him. This is not in the least so, although the only way to steer clear of further unpleasantness is to keep out of the way of the prison authorities, so we have hardly anything to do with them. We seek nothing from them, we do not want them to like us and we expect no good from them. That is why I do not want Ruth to make any request to Grant. I wrote to her twice telling her not to, because she would only humiliate herself.

'And do not think that you need be sorry for us all the time. We alternate work and study every day. The work is not difficult and we set our own pace, more or less. The convict in charge is easy-going, and as we know the job he leaves us alone. At eleven o'clock we go back to our room and eat some halva, olives or yoghourt and drink hot water (we usually manage to colour it and sweeten it a bit). Then we go out for an hour's exercise. In the afternoon we sit and study until three, and then we have a meal and lie down afterwards and read. In the evening we get more food, and sometimes a newspaper. We read until nine and then go to sleep. Sometimes we talk late into the night, and even the inspections—when a count is taken seven times every 24 hours, to see we are all here—do not bother us.

'The cold weather is over and our blankets and uniforms are certainly adequate. Compared with the other prisoners we are well off. We can see the sea and the beautiful view, and what more can one expect here? The only snag is that visits are such a bad business. For that reason alone we would like to be transferred to Athlit, because every Arab who comes to Acre from there reports that visiting at Athlit is easier and that the attitude is more humane.

'Just the same, things are not so terrible. Dad, what are the Government up to with their searches? Do they want to destroy the Yishuv? And do not forget to let me know well in advance and wait for my reply, if you want to pay a special visit, because otherwise it will not come off.'

12th February. Moshe wrote: 'I have nothing against those who are looking after our affairs now, but they are not the right men for the job. We need someone who will get to the point straightaway and arrange matters directly with the Commandant or his deputy. They are ready to listen and receive requests and suggestions. We are not even accorded our full rights. Books sent to us go astray en route and our visiting times have been cut by half.

'These things must be seen to. Since nobody asked our advice, we assumed that people outside know how to go about rectifying the situation, but in over four months they have not succeeded in organising the Jewish policemen here. No arrangements have been made with their superiors either, a sure sign that nobody knows how to do so. Meanwhile, life goes on somehow.'

5th April. The boys were moved to a camp in Misra'a. Ruth, Yael, Devora and I went to Misra'a to visit Moshe. We were allowed to see him in his room. He clung to Yael and kissed her. We all kissed each other, and then we left Moshe alone with Ruth —and a policeman. He looked well and was in good spirits. When we left the boys followed us with their eyes, and we parted sadly.

A week ago Ruth and Yael and I went to visit Mordechai Namirovsky. As we entered the prison yard we saw Moshe, accompanied by an Arab policeman. Yael instinctively ran over to her father and clasped him round the leg, but he pushed her aside and continued on his way across the yard as if he were a complete stranger. I can imagine how he must have felt then.

January,1941. Moshe wrote: 'We have been transferred to another camp. It is more comfortable than the first one, but I do not think we shall be here long because conditions are "too good for us here". If we are sent back I shall not be sorry, because this camp has drawbacks too. Meanwhile we are living, taking exercise, studying and sleeping, especially sleeping.

'In the last few days many Arab political prisoners have been released, but I have already ceased to pay any more attention to the matter. I am sure that the High Commissioner would still keep us in prison, even if he released all the criminals.

'Dov Hos was also pessimistic last time he was here. He did not think there was any chance of our being released unless energetic action were taken at the London end. What will happen now that Dov has been killed? He had no deputy to help him deal with our affairs. We had grown so close to him while we have been in prison that he was almost a member of the family. You cannot imagine what a dreadful effect the news of his death had on us.'

They were released about a month later, and many of the people who had shared our troubles came to share our joy. Aharon Meskin, Hanna Rovina and Shimon Finkel wrote on behalf of Habima:

'Accept our hearty good wishes on the return of your son Moshe to his home and to a life of work and freedom. We share in your joy. May his release in these days of stress be the harbinger of better times for us and for the world at large.'

As for me, a long time was to pass before I was free of the nightmare feeling which had haunted me during those months, and which had caused so much suffering to the boys who had been imprisoned.

At the time of the trial Ben-Gurion was Chairman of the Jewish Agency, and since the formation of the State of Israel has been Prime Minister and Minister of Defence. He kept a private diary, and Shmuel Dayan persuaded him to allow parts of it to be published in this volume, as it throws light on the official stand of both the British and Zionist leaders. The following passages, therefore, are quoted from the diaries of David Ben-Gurion.

Jerusalem, 11th October, 1939. I held consultations with Joseph, Gordon and Dov on the question of assistance for the Acre prisoners. We decided that Joseph should see Ritchie. We will suggest that we will help to prevent similar happenings in future if the present matter is dropped. Joseph will not offer any information in view of the fact that we have not had any meetings with the imprisoned boys and we do not know their story. We will assure the Government that from the names of the boys concerned it is clear they are not members of any terrorist group.

Jerusalem, 12th October, 1939. I came up to Jerusalem this morning to discuss the Acre prisoners with Joseph. He saw Ritchie yesterday evening and had a long talk about the matter. Ritchie began by being hostile but ended up by becoming quite friendly. He complained that our representative in Galilee had

XII. Moshe Dayan as a prisoner in Acre 1940, a
year before he lost one eye in Syria in the War.

XIII. Behind the plough on my farm at Nahalal in 1946.

XIV. My son, Moshe, with his wife Ruth and children, Assaf, Ehud, and Yael, in Jerusalem in 1950.

XV. Winter, 1957;
Moshe was C.-in-C. of
the Israeli army.

XVI. With my grand-
daughter Yael in the
Parliament restaurant,
1955.

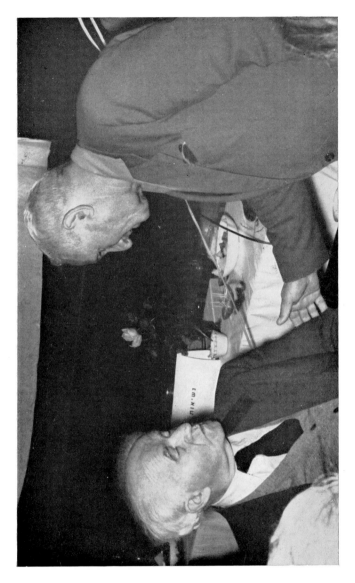

XVII. With Prime Minister David Ben-Gurion at Nahalal, 1957.

XVIII. Lecturing at a party meeting.

XIX. Degania today.

XX. Nahalal today.

not prevented such an operation and that they had not told the Government about it. He as good as indicated that this affair will result in arms searches at Jewish settlements. Joseph's explanations went a little way towards reassuring him and he promised to pass them on to the G.O.C.

Tel Aviv, 12th October, 1939. The arrest of the 43 boys near Yavniel a week ago is liable to interfere with the mobilisation plan. Apart from that, it is a very serious business because they are expected to be tried before a military court. In Government circles it is claimed that there is great disquiet among the Arabs

(*a*) because of the mobilisation carried out by the Jews,

(*b*) because of the parades held in Tel Aviv, and

(*c*) because of the Yavniel affair.

The attitude of the administration towards us is well known, and this latest event is bound to be exploited to hinder the organisation of the Division.

Jerusalem, 15th October, 1939. After the meeting, Ben-Zvi told me in the name of Rutenberg, who is ill at present, that Barker met him in the hotel on October 4th and complained that I keep sending him letters through a laywer instead of going to see him. He also heard from Kisch that Barker was complaining about it. I showed Ben-Zvi the letters that had passed between the G.O.C. and me, which made it quite clear that there had been some misunderstanding.

Jerusalem, 17th October, 1939. At 9.30 Dayan and Dinaburg, two of the parents, again came to see me about the arrested boys. Dayan asked if it would not be worth his going to England to get Dr. Weizmann to take action. I told him that I had no hope of preventing the trial from taking place, because the Palestine authorities did not treat us properly. The Army on the other hand was not unfriendly towards us and never had been, even in the worst days—quite the opposite, in fact. In London they would say that it was a judicial matter and that they could not intervene before the trial had taken place. Since, however, such a journey can do no harm, and the parents' feelings must be taken into account, especially those of the mothers, it is desirable that he should go to London.

Jerusalem, 30th October, 1939. After the meeting there was deputation after deputation. The first was of mothers and wives

K

of the 43, whose sentences were announced this morning. There were complaints about the conduct of the case, the lawyers, and the Jewish Agency Executive. Even though the complaints were unjustified they were understandable as an expression of the bitterness in people's hearts. We agreed that a deputation of wives and mothers should wait on the G.O.C. We informed them that we were considering what further steps could be taken.

Jerusalem, 31st October, 1939. Immediately afterwards there was another deputation from Tel Aviv—Berl Katzenelson, Sprinzak, Kossoy and Feinstein, accompanied by Dayan. They had also come about the 43 and demanded action in London and here. They suggested that someone should be sent to London immediately. I said that although it was clear that London would not intervene, we had agreed from the very beginning that Dayan should go to London and so put the parents' minds at rest. However, no visa had been forthcoming and it was doubtful whether anyone would manage to get to London before the G.O.C. had dealt with the matter finally. Therefore it was better to cable Chaim (Weizmann) and ask him to do what he could in the matter. Here in Palestine all that can be done is to appeal to the Commander-in Chief, and this the Agency and the Va'ad Leumi will do. It is also desirable that Dov should do so in the name of the Histadrut. No public action can be taken until the final sentences have been announced. According to my information the final sentences may be announced on Friday, though this is not certain.

Jerusalem, 1st November, 1939. At noon I had a meeting with the G.O.C. in the Army offices at the King David hotel. Our talk lasted an hour. Ritchie and the officer who acts as their Chief of Protocol were also there.

I thanked the G.O.C. for giving me the opportunity of discussing the distressing matter of the 43. I had no complaints about the military court, which was properly conducted in the normal manner. However, I wanted to raise with him two factors which I thought should be taken into account when the final sentence was determined.

First of all, I knew some of the accused men personally. I understood the type of person all 43 were. I was the last person to demand discrimination between Jew and Arab or between

Jews and any other people, but to my mind it was necessary to distinguish between robber or terrorist bands and honest working men who wanted only to defend themselves, and had no intention of harming anybody else. The 43 belonged to this latter category, although there was no doubt that in this instance they had broken the law. Not only that, but their action had been ill-considered in view of conditions in the country. Nevertheless, there could be no doubt whatever that these men did not want to attack anyone. Knowing the sort of people they were, it was inconceivable to anyone that they would ever use their weapons for criminal purposes.

In the trial the facts had been almost undisputed, except in the case of the boy sentenced to life imprisonment. Although I was not there I was certain, knowing these men as I did, that it was impossible that he had aimed a rifle at anybody. The G.O.C. interrupted me and said: 'You were in the Army. You know that every soldier can tell very well whether anyone is aiming a rifle at him or not.'

I replied: 'I do not wish to accuse anybody of not telling the truth. Just the same I am convinced that not one of the 43 aimed a rifle at anybody. Still, I did not come to argue about details. The main thing is that when these men's case is being considered the human factor must be taken into account, and so must motives.

'The second point I wish to raise is this: Together with all my fellow members of the Zionist leadership I have done my very best to educate the public to co-operate fully with England. We have done so for more than twenty years. The Jewish public in Palestine, of which the 43 are part, volunteered for the British army in the first World War. There has been co-operation with England all through the years. When the White Paper was issued we were forced, to our regret, to end our co-operation with the Government, but even then we told the public that it must realise the difference between opposition to a particular policy of the British Government and its general attitude to England.

'I do not need to tell you how we hate the policy of the White Paper, but we have still continued to co-operate with the British Army in Palestine in maintaining law and order. I returned to Palestine before the War broke out. When we heard that England had declared war, we made the following public proclamation: "Although the White Paper has been issued, and we shall have to continue to fight for our rights in this country, the war against Hitler has faced us with graver questions. We shall all stand by England in this war as one man." The Jewish public in Palestine has responded to our call. The 43 who have been imprisoned belonged to this category, and that factor should be taken into account when the illegal act they have committed is being judged.'

The G.O.C. said that he did not wish to talk about the matter with anybody until after the trial. He had not yet gone into the matter thoroughly but had merely glanced through all the documents for the purpose of our conversation, so that he would know what we were talking about. Although he himself had overall responsibility in the matter he had passed on to his subordinates the job of examining the various legal points in detail. He felt constrained to say that this was the most serious thing that had happened in Palestine since the war started, and that he had found it necessary to hold consultations on the matter with the High Commissioner for the last two days. He had told the Commissioner about his forthcoming meeting with me, and the Commissioner agreed with him that he should ask me whether I had come to see him in my capacity as an official representative of the Jewish Agency or just as one of the country's notables.

I replied: 'I did not consider the matter at all before coming to see you. If you wish to speak to me in my capacity as Chairman of the Jewish Agency, please do so. If on the other hand you wish to regard me as just another Palestinian Jew I am perfectly agreeable.'

He returned to the subject several times, emphasising that the character of our talk would depend on the capacity in which I had come to see him, because if I had come as a person of importance in the Yishuv he would not be able to ask me the sort of questions he could ask the head of the Jewish Agency. I told him that I was a representative of the Agency, that he could ask me any question he liked, and that I would answer his questions to the best of my ability.

He said that my claim that these men were decent people meant nothing. This had been said during the trial as well. What mattered was what they had done. The facts were quite clear.

There was no doubt that they were armed and were carrying out military training in order to form an army. It was clear that the aim of this was a rebellion against England. From a personal point of view they were doubtless decent men, but so were most revolutionaries in their private lives.

The argument that had been advanced at the trial, that these men had worked with the army, the police and the other services, and this was to their credit, was the weakest point of their entire defence. In fact, this very point was to their discredit. It showed that these men had taken Government jobs in order to acquire knowledge which would be useful for their revolutionary plans. The G.O.C. had become very excited and was speaking more loudly than usual, so that it was not easy for me to interrupt him with my answer.

I said: 'Although I do not dispute the fact that these men were armed, and that they were apparently engaged in military training, this cannot in any way be considered as proof that they were building up an army or preparing a rebellion. These allegations are pure supposition and there is not an iota of proof in support of them. From my knowledge of these men I am certain that they are not revolutionaries and they cannot be regarded as intending any action against England.'

He did not let me say any more, but broke in: 'I am an army man, and I know. Some of you are exceptionally able speakers but I look at things simply. I was sent here to maintain law and order in the country. I am doing so and shall continue to do so. I will not allow people to bring in weapons from abroad and arm themselves in secret. I cannot allow a private army to be created here. In England it would be considered high treason. It must be eliminated, and I wish to ask you if you are ready to assist us.'

I replied: 'With the very greatest respect, I am sorry but I must reject your allegation about the aims of these 43 men. I cannot deny that there are groups of men with illegal arms in Palestine, but there are reasons for this:

'(a) For years, in Turkish times and unfortunately even after the country was conquered from them, we have had to defend ourselves. The Government cannot guarantee our lives, so it is no wonder that in such a situation—which has lasted for many, many years—there are Jews in Palestine who have seen to it that they should have arms. However, I must point out, and I suppose you know this as well, that the Jews have never used their weapons to attack anybody. The last four years have been proof of that. Women, children and old people have been murdered, but we have always told the Jewish public: "Do not take the law into into your own hands. We shall limit ourselves to self-defence and we demand that the Government arm us so that we can defend ourselves." I am happy to say that the Government heeded our request to some extent and we vvere thus enabled to prevent the Jewish public from taking the law into its own hands. Nobody can claim that our men used their arms to attack anybody. Of course, there were a few exceptions and a very small section of the public did not listen to us. But I know the 43, and they do not belong to this minority, or its organisation, and they do not share its ideas.

'(b) The second reason that can impel Jewish youth to acquire military training is without a doubt the desire to take part, if there should be need, in the war against Hitler on the side of England.'

The G.O.C. interrupted me and said: 'Those rifles were brought into this country before the War. You cannot claim that this was done in order to co-operate in the war against Germany.' I replied that I could not say anything about bringing arms into the country. It must certainly have been before the War, and there was no doubt that they were for defence purposes.

The G.O.C. asked: 'What is the name of the organisation to which the men belong?' I said: 'I do not know if they belong to any organisation, but I know the name you are thinking of. In Hebrew it is "Hagana" (I saw the word written in English on a piece of paper in front of him).

'Yes, yes, "Hagana," that's it,' he said. I told him: 'I know that this mistake is one commonly made by the English here who do not understand Hebrew. This word is not a proper name, but the Hebrew word "defence".'

'Men in possession of grenades cannot belong to "defence",' the G.O.C. said. 'They should call themselves "attack". Tell me, please how do you say "attack" in Hebrew?' I told him, and he turned to Ritchie and said: 'Write down that name. That is what the underground organisation should be called.' Then he turned to me: 'Men who arm themselves in secret are infringing the law, and so working against the Government. Yet you testify that their purpose is to aid the Government.'

I said: 'I admit that these men were found with weapons in their possession and there is no doubt that they were breaking the law, but not every infringement of the law signifies opposition to the Government. In this country there are many people who have weapons without permission. Everybody knows that some of the Arabs who used to belong to gangs have left them and surrendered a few weapons to the Government. They have promised the Government that they will oppose the gangs, and walk about armed, even though they have no licences for their weapons.'

The G.O.C. asked me to name some of these Arabs and I did so. He then said that if this were true they would be arrested the very next day. I said that I had nothing against them and had not come to ask him to arrest them. I had merely wanted to show that there were people who had unlicensed weapons and the Government tolerated this if it knew that these weapons would not be used for illegal purposes.

'I will not allow anybody to have unauthorised weapons,' the G.O.C. retorted.

I told him: 'Up till now we have helped as much as we could to maintain law and order. How have we done this? We are not a Government, we are not strong. All we can do is to bring moral influence to bear.' 'You are strong, all right,' Barker broke in.

'I wish we were! Our only strength is moral strength. We have brought this to bear and shall continue to do so, so that the Jewish public knows how to defend itself, but it has never attacked anybody. Even when it was itself under attack it restricted itself to self-defence. The behaviour of the Jewish public in these difficult times was, I am sure, of great assistance to the Government in their efforts to maintain order. But we would not have been able to help at all if you had prevented us from defending ourselves. If we had had no means of self-defence, I doubt whether they would have listened to us. They would have taken the law into their own hands. Our co-operation with you depends on your behaviour towards us,' I told him.

'Are you trying to tell me that if we give you arms you will aid us, and if not, you will not?' he asked. 'I am only a soldier and as a soldier I have the duty to ensure that nothing is done here against the law. I must eliminate all illegal organisations unconditionally, I will do so, and it will be to your advantage also. I have been here only a few months and I do not know how much longer I shall be here, but you and your men will still be here even after another fifty years, and you will want law and order here in Palestine.'

I said that nobody wanted law and order more than we did, but that the Jews must always be able to defend themselves, and we would rather it was with the consent and assistance of the English. 'It is obvious,' I concluded, 'that our co-operation with the Army depends on your behaviour towards the Jews in Palestine.'

We all stood up, and as I was leaving, he said: 'I am a soldier. It is my duty to maintain law and order and I will do so.'

On my way out I saw Agronsky in the waiting room. He told me that he had an appointment with the G.O.C. at one o'clock. He had met Barker before, in London, and a few days ago had sent Barker a note asking to see him.

When I returned to the office I was informed that Rutenberg had come out of the G.O.C.'s room before I went in. Rutenberg told me practically nothing about his conversation, but I heard an account of it second-hand from Joseph, who saw him immediately afterwards. As far as I could make out he had kept the matter on a political level and the G.O.C. gave him much the same sort of answers as he had given me.

I cabled to Moshe Shertok: 'I saw the G.O.C. this morning about the convicted men. I had intended to discuss the matter from a personal viewpoint, but he directed the conversation along political lines, after having had consultations on the matter with the Commissioner. From what he said it is clear that he regards these men as part of an illegal, armed organisation which is preparing a rebellion against England. I had the distinct impression that this is due to the Commissioner's influence. He asked for aid in uncovering the organisation and its arms. There will be searches. It seems that M.M.'s policy (Malcolm Macdonald, Secretary for the Colonies) is being introduced in the realm of security as well.'

Jerusalem, 5th November, 1939. I went up to Jerusalem. The expected Executive Committee meeting was not held this morning, so Rutenberg asked me to arrange it for Monday, so that he could be present.

Despite a telegram from London notifying us of his date of arrival, Berl Locker has still not arrived. In the meantime there has been disquieting news. Army circles made the following suggestions to London the day before yesterday:

(a) To give the Jewish organisations a severe warning that they must disband the illegal organisations and hand in all illegal arms by a certain date.

(b) If this demand is not complied with, to reduce drastically the number of Jewish auxiliaries and dismiss Jews attached to British Army units.

(c) To ban all military exercises, whether with or without weapons.

(d) To institute systematic searches of Jews for weapons.

They know that such a course of action could have grave consequences, but they are prepared to suffer them.

On the same day, civilian circles in London informed us that they had had extended consultations with the Army about the 43. The G.O.C. has not yet taken a decision, wishing to consider the matter further, but the 43 are not as important as what has happened because of them—the discovery of a secret armed force, which although its existence had been suspected had never been *proved* to exist. Nor had there been proof of any operations on its part. Now the Government will have to decide on its course of action. There are three possibilities:

(a) To find the arms and eradicate the organisation by force. This step is logical, and is the correct one to take in the Government's opinion. It would also be popular in Arab circles. On the other hand such a move would strike at the very roots of Jewish aspirations and engender fierce opposition, destroying Jewish co-operation and causing a renewal of Jewish terrorism. Furthermore, it would have repercussions among world Jewry and influence the war situation.

(b) They could ignore the entire affair. This would be convenient, but it has already been made public, and to drop it now would mean loss of face. Such a step would encourage the Jews, anger the Arabs, and also affect the war situation.

(c) They could decide on a course of action half-way between the first two. This would not provoke the Jews or the Arabs and would permit a reduction in the number of auxiliaries. The High Commissioner is in favour of (c), and has made the following suggestions to the G.O.C.

i If there is reliable information about arms being concealed in particular places, they should be searched. The behaviour of those making the search must be circumspect, in order to avoid undesirable incidents.

ii Illegal training and exercises must be stopped, under the Emergency Regulations.

iii The number of Jewish auxiliaries must be reduced appreciably because of what was revealed at the trial.

iv Systematic searches should not be carried out in Jewish towns and villages.

i and iii are likely to lead to clashes, but there can be no retreat. The G.O.C. considers that only i will be effective in liquidating the organisation, but is willing to consider the Commissioner's views.

In the meantime our comrades in London made representations to the Government. They argued that:

1. It is an open secret in Palestine that the Jews, particularly in areas of agricultural settlement, possess illegal arms for defence purposes. In the course of visits by army and police officers to Jewish settlements in order to inspect their defence plans, this has been mentioned more than once. In several cases the authorities *knew* that Jews were only able to beat off attacks because of their illegal arms. The attack on Tirat Zvi in 1938 is a case in point. Government help came too late, and every officer in the area knew that the settlement had been saved from destruction because two grenades had been thrown.

2. There are many illegal arms in the country. The Arabs use theirs for attack, the Jews for defence. Throughout all the years of disturbances, very, very few Jews used their weapons for revenge. Certainly there was no thought of revenge in the minds of the 43. The place where they were arrested is in

an area of Jewish settlement, where there has never been a case of any Jew making an attack.

3. All the men sentenced at the trial have clean records. Many were auxiliaries, like Dayan of Nahalal. Others served in the Special Night Squads and fought against terrorist bands in the most dangerous area, like Zvi Brenner of Afikim. They might have used their weapons for training, or defence, or in preparation for service with the British Army, but never in any circumstances for crime.

Before the carrying of arms was made a punishable offence under army regulations, talks were held with the then G.O.C. Wavell in 1937, and the question was raised with him, of the danger in which Jews would be placing themselves if they were found in possession of arms even though they did not intend to use them for terrorist activities. Wavell promised then that the Army would always examine the intentions of anyone found carrying arms. This promise invalidates the prosecutor's argument at the trial that the intentions of the person found in possession of a weapon are irrelevant. Jewish defence in Palestine is not only static. There is also mobile defence and for this reason the Jews must be allowed to carry out field training. The attack on Maon in 1938 was beaten off only because the defenders had had that kind of training.

The Jewish Agency does not seek to justify infractions of the law, but an injustice will have been perpetrated if intentions similar to those of the members of marauding bands should be ascribed to the 43. The whole Yishuv identifies itself with the 43, and confirmation of the sentences is likely to have grave consequences.

Jerusalem, 6th November, 1939. This morning there was a meeting of the Executive. I reported on the political situation, the talks with the G.O.C. and the intentions of the Government. I informed the Executive that I had reached the conclusion that I ought to go to London for a few days to report on the situation to Weizmann before he leaves for America, and to consult with our colleagues in London on what is to be done if the Government takes the action it is threatening to take. Everyone except S. considered my journey to be necessary.

Jerusalem, 8th November, 1939. The question of the 43 has

been taken up with Butler, Attlee and Sinclair. Cazalet, who has joined up and is in anti-aircraft defence, happens to be in the same office as Wingate and is very active in the matter.

Tel Aviv, 9th November, 1939 .At 7 o'clock this morning, Reuven came and told me that M.M. had told his representative in Jerusalem, that the important question raised as a result of the trial will be considered by a small committee, and that therefore the sentences on the 43 should be confirmed. In the meantime L. has expressed his agreement with most of the suggestions put forward by the G.O.C. The only thing he opposes is a prior approach to the Jewish institutions.

I left Tel Aviv with a heavy heart. When I reached Haifa at 10 a.m., I immediately went to the *Ala Littoria* offices. They told me there that the plane would not be leaving till the next morning because of bad weather. I decided to stay in Haifa and see various people. I immediately got in touch with Biram, and went to see him at the Reali School. I suggested that he should agree to become head of Mishmar Ha'am, but he refused. Apart from his work at the Reali he devoted all his spare time to a training school, he said, and had no time left for anything else, much as Mishmar Ha'am attracted him.

London, 13th November, 1939. As soon as I arrived at the Mount Royal Hotel I telephoned the office, and was told that Moshe was not there, as he had gone to meet me. After a few minutes Lourie telephoned me and told me that Chaim had an appointment with Butler at 5.30 and wanted to see me immediately. The next moment Moshe came in. He had missed my arrival and had just returned from the Imperial Airways office. We both hurried to the Dorchester, where Weizmann was staying, and found him ready to leave. We went with him by car as far as the Foreign Office, and I gave him a brief account of the measures the Government were preparing to take as a result of the trial of the 43. Weizmann was furious. We left him at the Foreign Office.

An hour and a half later Weizmann gave us a summary of the talk he had had with Butler. What he told Butler had impressed him very much, and he had promised to pass it all on to Halifax that same evening. He had advised Chaim to have a meeting with Ironside, the Chief of the General Staff, so Chaim telephoned him and made an appointment for 4 o'clock next day. He also suggested that I should see M.M. so that he would not be able to complain that things were being done behind his back, because Ministers could only take action on something after the Ministry concerned had been consulted. At nine in the evening we had a meeting with Chaim at his hotel. I gave a more detailed report of the situation in Palestine and the hostile policy of M.M. and his representative. Chaim reported in detail on his talk with Butler and asked me to have a meeting with M.M. I said that such a meeting would be damaging politically, and that my heart was not in it. Chaim said that we could consider the matter next morning.

London, 14th November, 1939. This morning we had news from Palestine that the G.O.C. had decided to reduce the sentences passed on the 43. Theo's was cut to ten years, and the others' to five.

At a meeting in Chaim's room this morning I reported on the news from Palestine and asked that we should consider what ought to be done about it. Chaim was not prepared to do this. He said that during the night he had thought about the meeting with M.M., and had come to the conclusion that a Jew could not refuse to meet even the devil if it should be necessary. He did not hope for much from a meeting with Malcolm, but failure to see him could hinder us in our approach to the rest of the Cabinet. I said that I would do as Chaim said, even though I disagreed with him.

London, 15th November, 1939. At this morning's meeting Chaim reported on his talk with Ironside. The Chief of Staff had been sincere and friendly. He had already read all the documents and considered the sentences harsh as well as foolish. He had already cabled to Barker to reduce them and review them again in six months' time. Among other things, he said: 'Fancy, they have condemned one of Wingate's lads to life imprisonment. He ought to have been given the D.S.O.' Ironside expressed the opinion that mobilisation of the Jews in Palestine was sure to come.

15th November, 1939. I had a meeting with M.M. at the Colonial Office at 4 p.m. It was a most unpleasant meeting. Malcolm greeted me with a smile and was very friendly. As soon as I started to speak the smile disappeared and his face grew stern. I told him that I had not come to talk about the 43 young men

who had been sentenced to long terms of imprisonment. Worse
things were happening to Jews then than unjust imprisonment.
I had come to discuss the political matters bound up with the case.

I felt in duty bound to caution the Government not to disarm
the Jews without consideration beforehand of the results of such
an action. If our arms were taken away it would be regarded as
encouragement by the Arabs to attack the Jews, and they would
all be massacred.

We had not always blamed the British Government when
something had happened to us in Palestine, but this time if they
were to take away our arms and something were to happen, the
British Government would be responsible, because we had
warned them in time.

I got up to go, but Malcolm asked me to stay a moment because
he had one last observation to make: 'You said that the sentences
on the 43 young men were political. I can assure you that neither
the Government in London nor the High Commissioner gave
any instructions to the military court. On the contrary, as soon
as we heard the arguments you put forward we transmitted them
to the High Commissioner.'

London, 16th November, 1939. In the morning I had a meeting
with Orde Wingate. I consulted him on questions likely to arise
out of the trial of the 43. He, of course, is in favour of continuing
operations and taking a strong stand against any attempts at
disarming the Jews in Palestine. Orde is convinced that there
will be a Jewish army in Palestine. He has no doubt that Italy will
come into the war, that the Near East will become a battlefield
and that then they will have need of us.

16th November, 1939. While I was with Wingate, Chaim and
Moshe happened to meet McLeod. He told them that Ironside
had sent a cable immediately after he had received the documents
from Wavell.

In his opinion there had been no need to try the 43. The western
defences in Europe would be difficult to breach, so the Germans
would thrust southwards. England would need a military base in
the Near East. There would be a Jewish army.

The army in the east could not depend on a supply line running
all the way back to England. When the drive southward came,
the Jews would fulfil their duty. At the moment the Chief of

Staff was trying to overcome the opposition of the Ministry of Supply. When he had done so, he would have to face the opposition of the Colonial Office and would overcome that too! Chaim told him about the idea for a division and also about my talk with Malcolm.

The entry above was the last one dealing with the 43. The diary of David Ben-Gurion, written for his own use and not originally intended for publication, demonstrates his personal courage and the strong stand he took against the authorities in Palestine. His words were received as if he were the representative of a powerful, independent nation, not a group of people only 400,000 strong. All this was at a time when Hitlerite Germany was exterminating the Jews of Europe, and when the Arab rebellion against us had caused many gaps in our ranks.

His spiritual strength lay in the vision that possessed his soul. He was fired by the truth and righteousness of our struggle, and by his deep faith that we would overcome every obstacle in our path.

Even when doubt gnawed at our hearts, he knew how to rally the remnants of our strength against those who wanted to destroy us. This was the path he trod throughout those dark days for the Diaspora abroad and the Yishuv in Palestine, and he did not swerve from it until victory was won.

CHAPTER FIVE

NEW IMMIGRANTS: A NEW BEGINNING

The state was established, the war won. To many people it was the end of a struggle and the start of a comfortable life. For Shmuel Dayan it was a new beginning.

The responsibilities the state produced were perhaps less exciting, and at times less practical, but definitely not less important or demanding. The child had been born and it needed a nurse, parents, teachers.

Shmuel Dayan never regarded the state as an end in itself, and 1949 was a new start, as the establishment of Degania or Nahalal had been. He was elected to the Knesset (the Israeli Parliament) but this was never his only occupation; his main work was with the new immigrants, for whom the moshav was the only possible way of life and who desperately needed help. Once again it was necessary to create the 'New Jew.' But in 1908 the settlers were enthusiastic pioneers; in 1950 they were generally inexperienced and elderly newcomers.

There was one solution—the second generation, the integrated children of the 1908 pioneers. It was their turn now to lead, teach and advise, and they did so.

Shmuel Dayan, today still one of the moshav leaders, gives an account of his encounter with the new immigrants. Being by nature a field worker he never operated in an office. From village to village, the south and the north, never weary or complaining, he started a new routine of life—a few days in Parliament, a few in the new villages, and the weekends at Nahalal, his village. Thus he was not only among the people who established Nahalal and Degania, but among those who inspired and helped a whole movement, hundreds of villages, thousands of people.

Here again, the political implications are not included. The party, Ben-Gurion's Mapai, is only mentioned. This is the account of a man who worked, not because he had to, but because he felt he wanted to, and enjoyed it and loved it.

In June 1954, Ben-Gurion was present at a Moshav Youth Congress held at Nahalal. The people of Nahalal gathered at the entrance to the village to welcome him. They regarded him, and still do, as their elder brother, the one whose thought and vision paved the way for them and transformed even those of little faith into believers and men of action. Those who had worked with him at various settlements in 1906 and 1907 had a special reason for wanting to shake his hand.

It was a Saturday when Ben-Gurion addressed the Congress in the communal hall. A thousand people packed it to capacity and crowds stood outside to listen to his speech. He said:

'Comrades, many of you, like myself, are no strangers to congresses and meetings. However, I cannot remember any occasion when it was so difficult to come and say what has to be said here and now. This is not merely one more Jewish settlement in Israel: we are gathered here in a place that has been and always will be a symbol of the Jewish people's pioneering values. There is another place like this one in Israel, one that is as much of a symbol to our youth, and I think that some of its founders are here today. I refer to Degania. These two places achieved the utmost demanded of them. Their members came to this country, they came to work, they came to build Hebrew culture, they came to work on the land and be independent, they came to do agricultural work on the basis of mutual help, and in their daily lives they achieved the most that anyone could have demanded from himself or from anyone else.

'If we had time we could do things slowly. If someone could guarantee that we could stay here in peace and security for fifty years, we should be able to do the job gradually. We could say:

"We shall wait twenty years, for this is the generation of the wilderness and there is nothing to hope for from them. We shall rear children, they will go to our schools, afterwards they will serve in the Israel Defence Forces, and then they will be like us." And they *will* be like us! But we cannot do this. We have no guarantee that we shall have scores of years of peace. And since there is not time, and we are under pressure, and there are few to act and those few do but little—this is not enough.

'Why do I say that the few have done but little? Because they came as guides. We must train the new citizens who have come to this country. We must approach them as brothers, and be as one with them. Only then shall we be able to spread among the new immigrants that spirit that we have inherited. They are Jews like us and they have the ability to acquire the same characteristics as us—the positive ones. We have not helped them to do this.

'I consider that the settlement of immigrants in the Negev and perhaps later in the corridor, is the means of attaining a more distant goal. This goal is not yet clear to me, but what *is* clear is that the situation in the country must be changed. We believe that if we maintain the impetus of the wave of enthusiasm sweeping over us today, we shall be justified in asking others to accompany us. I do not consider that it would be at all a bad thing if the call went out from here to the youth—at least of the Ihud—to accompany us, nor do I think it would be undesirable for the people of the kibbutzim to become instructors in new immigrant settlements. If we sound the call and then act, others will follow in our footsteps.

'Today a new generation must arise, in addition to the old generation. It must enter into the life of the State in the field of settlement, of security, of the economy and of morals.'

Representatives of the youth also spoke, as did the then Chief of Staff, Moshe Dayan, and Levi Eshkol, Minister of Finance. In my own speech I tried to emphasise the sense of continuity created by the Youth Congress at Nahalal. I said:

'Since the establishment of the State in 1948 we have scrapped the original policy, in the Agricultural Centre and other institutions, of beginning the settlement of new immigrants as they are, without any sort of preparation. First, Nahalal and Kfar

Vitkin and other settlements have worked and lived with immigrants in their settlements. Mothers and fathers from the older settlements, some two hundred of them, have answered the call, and they are proud that some of their children have also obeyed this inner urge and are prepared to carry on what has been begun. This is a great achievement. A spirit of this kind does not exist in just any town. It cannot be found in any other movement, or in the city. We are happy and proud of this fact and we wish to work together in an organised manner with moshav councils, and the moshav movements, because this operation demands organisation.

'We can assume that the matter will be looked at askance in many moshavim and that there will be problems which may well divide parents and children. I am sure that there are no divisions of opinion on matters of principle that cannot be resolved. The moshav movement will convene the council, which will consider every problem and find the correct solution to it.

'We must say to everyone: "If you are about fifty years of age, or if you have a son or an older brother or sister, one of the family must go." What we must avoid doing, of course, is depopulating the village or ruining the farm economy we have built up together, fathers and sons, over tens of years. It has served as an example to new immigrants and to the State as a whole. We have not created a settlement that lives by exploiting the workers, and we do not wish to do so. We do not have to neglect our fields and ruin our economy. We can carry out the operation we all want without doing so.

'We cannot wait until a committee is set up to carry out this operation and inspire wider circles to co-operate. Ben-Gurion has put the obligation on us to act now and publicise our aim throughout our movement, in the moshavim, the kibbutzim and the cities. A start has been made in this moshav and we shall continue along this path.

'We have been bringing up our people as socialists for nearly fifty years, and where are the results? We cannot set up four settlements with a hundred or even two hundred people. Even five hundred will not be enough for the task.

'The principal point raised yesterday evening by Ben-Gurion is that of the security of our frontiers. We must set up settlements

L*

of our youth. Tens of thousands of young people must settle there. Our party and the workers' federation will take the first step. We shall leave the cities, the institutions and the Government services and go out to the borders! Our sons will go and Nahalal will be vindicated, and so will the moshav movement. Ben-Gurion, redeemer of the State of Israel, has said: "I knew that God was in this place." There is nothing higher than that.'

Some two hundred young people went out to the Negev to act as instructors in new immigrant settlements. Most of them came from Nahalal, Kfar Vitkin, and Kfar Yehoshua, with Nahalal providing the biggest proportion of all.

There were meetings and talks and conferences in the moshavim. Nobody was opposed to the idea. On the contrary, everybody was in favour of it, and fathers were proud of their children who were prepared to go to the Negev. Even though some of the parents who were over sixty did not see how they could carry on without young working hands to help them, and even though the sick and the very old had to be considered, the young people's decision was accepted.

After a farewell party fifty of Nahalal's young people set out for the Negev. Trees grew by the roadside—eucalyptus, acacia and others—helping by their growth to redeem the barren wastes. There were many settlements to be seen, big ones among them, with houses scattered among the fields, each house with its own plot of land. Although the trees had not yet grown enough to give shade and shelter to the houses, they were being tended by the settlers and would grow to their full height and spread. Farm buildings would be built, the farms would be extended, and every family would have space to grow. New immigrants were making the fields of the Negev flourish. Ground nuts, onions, maize—all were green and growing, while the irrigation sprinklers turned and turned. There was a goat tethered near every house, and in the centre of the village an extensive area had been deep ploughed.

The houses belonged to Yemenite settlers and they had already been furnished with cupboards, tables and chairs and beds. Some even had pictures on the walls. It was clear that all these families more than covered their expenses; they were saving money. Everybody looked fit and well.

A young Nahalal family occupied one of the unpretentious little houses in the centre of the village, reserved for skilled tradesmen. Curtains covered the windows, two babies were having their afternoon sleep in their cots, and a gentle wind blew, softening some of the heat of the afternoon. A young couple sat at the door of the house. They had arrived only the evening before from Nahalal. They looked up at the blue sky and then surveyed the quiet empty expanse all round them. Had they done the right thing? Their confidence that they had, showing in their eyes—would it last long?

The Negev, conquered for us by our sons, many of whom gave their lives for it, is a storehouse of riches. Nobody knows what its soil conceals. Its millions of dunams of land can support as large a population as the north of the country, if properly developed. And we cannot afford to delay its development. From the first day of its capture, Jews settled at Eilat and small groups went out to prospect the Arava. Many pioneering activities were begun —drilling for water, drilling for oil, iron and copper mining, the establishment of farms, chemical fertiliser manufacture, the Dead Sea potash works.

We are in a state of war, and the land is empty. There is no security for the workers in the Negev, for they are few and alone in this huge empty area. That is why we must extend our operations at once and conquer the empty spaces of the Negev so that safety can be assured for all who live and work there.

Some tens of settlements must be built in the Negev near places of employment and also near the Beersheba-Eilat road. Each one must be built either in the form of a watch tower, like the one that used to be at Beit Eshel, or else like the police stations of Mandatory times, with all the buildings inside a courtyard surrounded by a bullet-proof wall. At the beginning our youth will people these settlements, like the early days. They will earn their living by working on various development projects, and where water is found they can do experimental farming. Factories and other enterprises with easily transportable products will be transferred to the Negev. Garages and stores will be built along the roads, and trees planted, especially date palms.

All this will call for investment which will not yield an immediate return. Only in the distant future will returns begin to flow. We must use the Development Budget, reparations, and funds collected abroad for developing the Negev. The whole operation must be conceived as a war—a war against the desert. These investments are justified from the point of view of achieving security for everyone working in the Negev. Without them, even the amounts invested so far would be lost.

After the State had been established new immigrants settled in many places throughout Israel, including her borders, and brought neglected land into cultivation. But Israel's youth has not been fulfilling its principal duty—to people the country's waste lands. Our youth must leave the cities and forswear amusements and diversions, for the desert fields of Israel call! There these young people will discover themselves, and nature and the land will reflect their likeness. There is no time to lose. Guarding the Negev will be an important duty. It will be almost like joining the army, so the settlers must be young. The army itself must also be on guard in the Negev, the most important and at the same time the most difficult region of our State.

The gulf between veteran settlers and new immigrants was bridged by the people of Kfar Vitkin and Nahalal. They had conquered Emek Hefer and Emek Jezreel twenty-five years earlier, and now they wanted to forge solid links of aid and friendship with the settlers of Patish—new immigrants from Persia and Kurdistan, who had come to live in the Negev and conquer it through work. Varda, the daughter of Frooma and Israel Friedmann of Kfar Vitkin was murdered at Patish, the new immigrants' moshav. She had gone there as an instructor, to help the new settlers to organise their moshav the way her village was organised. She had gone with her comrades, other young people from other moshavim. Patish had been built in the middle of a wilderness with mountains all round. Each house had its own plot of ground, and the Kurdistanis and Persians moved in in 1949.

It was night-time and Patish was celebrating the wedding of two of its members. The bride and groom were staying on the outskirts of the moshav where no tree yet grew and everything was clearly visible. Everywhere in the village the lamps were lit and tables laid with food and drink. Everybody was celebrating and had cast care aside. They all formed a circle and began to dance.

The dance was an eastern one and Varda was unfamiliar with it, but she followed the movements of the others. As they danced, hands on each other's shoulders, a grenade burst in the centre of the circle. Twenty men and one woman were injured by splinters. Varda sank to the ground and did not rise again. The grenade had been thrown by marauders from across the Egyptian border. It was part of the minor war being waged against us, despite our victory in the War of Liberation.

Varda was buried in her native village and a girl from another moshav came to take her place. The inhabitants of Patish were confused and shocked by what had happened. The bandaged injured came back from hospital in Beersheba, thinking all the time about the security situation and about the young girl who had been killed. 'If only it had been one of us instead,' they said. 'After all, it is we who have inherited this land.'

At Patish the injured recovered, got up and went back to tending their land by day and standing guard at night. Their determination and their devotion to the defence of their mother-land was even greater now than before. The mother of one of the injured wanted to assure us that they would stand fast, so she put her hand on her heart and with great emotion said in her own language: 'The State of Israel is here, in my heart.'

One rainy night, Ben-Gurion had been speaking to a gathering of new immigrants in their own language. They were very excited, because this was the first time they had seen or heard the Prime Minister. We, the old hands, were also there and we listened as one of the new immigrants told his story:

'At the end of the war in Europe,' he said, 'I was riding across Russia on horseback together with a Russian, a non-Jew. Day and night we rode on, and during our long ride talked about many different subjects. One evening we came to a village, and my comrade the Russian soldier jumped off his horse and kissed the ground, not once but many times. "This is my land, my village!" he shouted, and disappeared among the houses. And I, the Jewish soldier, stayed on my horse, and asked myself, "Where is *my* land?" It was then that I decided to come to Israel.'

For us also the end of the war was in sight, and there was urgent need to consolidate our conquests and settle the country speedily. It was essential to create a soundly based economy and not indulge in wasteful expenditure, and to turn the battlefields into productive land. We wanted to send the soldier back to his plough, making him into a man who would build and create. A hundred thousand immigrants came to Israel, but only a small percentage moved to the country and an even smaller percentage joined agricultural settlements.

New settlements went up with speed and precision, but their inhabitants did not engage in agriculture. However, it was not enough just to come and live in Israel. The question was how to settle the whole country. And what sort of State was it going to be? We had always preached settlement on the land, but despite all the emissaries we had sent to the Diaspora over the years, Jews did not want to come and live in our village. What were we going to do? Our reserves of manpower for settlement amounted to thirty, and this included our youth. But there were millions of dunams of land to be settled. How could we get the Jews to settle on the land? We had to settle the border areas and we had to grow food, and both these things had to be done quickly. In the Negev, of course, it would be years before the land could yield crops; and many frontier areas were mountainous. There was only one thing to do—turn part of the Army into settlers. The farmers knew the secret of combining the two activities, and when their testing time had come they had made excellent soldiers. As for the interior of the country, all settlers who were in their forties must be absorbed into existing agricultural society so that within two or three years they would be able to see the fruits of their labours. Although we had no training farms, we could send instructors in various trades to every group of a hundred immigrants and within a year or two they would be farming their own land.

New immigrants in their forties do not want to settle on the land, but their reasons for refusing to do so are not quite clear. Perhaps it is because they have not received adequate spiritual preparation, or because life is easier in an immigrant camp than on the land. The fact is that immigrants run away back to the camps. Perhaps the time has come to compel every immigrant to settle on the land. It would not be a catastrophe for them. Each one would receive a house and land, and would have the chance of becoming a good farmer in time.

Today there are whole villages standing empty. True, the houses are only made of clay but they are better than those we lived in at Um-Juni years ago. New immigrants must be brought to see that they must live in the deserted villages, and they must be given no alternative. As for immigrant youth, we have become accustomed to regarding them as being interested only in amusement because they grew up in the days of Hitler. We are a poor people and we are faced with a gigantic task. We must divide immigrant youth up into groups of a hundred and put instructors and land at the disposal of every group. All the funds set aside for these young people must be spent on helping them become attached to the land and to Israel, and to make them self-reliant conquerors of the soil. We are confronted with a task we cannot carry out without young people, and the young people are available.

Mass settlement went ahead at an unprecedented pace, which justified our old decision to leave Degania and establish Nahalal. In five years most of what was needed for a farm had been provided—a small house (with an extra room for families with many children); a cowshed; a poultry house; enough piped water to irrigate ten dunams; tools and implements, including tractors, combines, seed drills and trucks; work animals for every three farm units; a cow and fifty chickens; seeds and fertilisers; and capital to enable the needs of the house and the farm to be covered for several months. The soil had been prepared by deep ploughing for the planting of fruit trees, vines or citrus, depending on soil conditions and the area.

Every family received thirty dunams of land, and eighty to a hundred-and-thirty farm units of this kind formed a village. The houses were fifty yards or so apart, and every settler could see his own land. Recently, matters have been arranged so that each house has ten dunams of land adjoining it. In each village there are also ten two-dunam plots for skilled tradesmen. These work at their trade, but have this small auxiliary farm and grow their own food.

In each village a feed store has been built, as well as shops, a dairy, a school, a kindergarten, a club, a health centre, and offices. Approach roads have been built to half the villages, connecting them with nearby main roads. Many villages have been linked up with the electricity supply. Half of them have telephones as well.

The Government has financed the building of living accommodation, as well as the roads and the telephone service. All the agricultural plant and equipment has been supplied by the Jewish Agency, most of whose funds have come from Government loans and from Zionist fund raising activities. The value of the equipment given to each settler varies between ten and twenty thousand pounds, which settlers have contracted to repay over thirty-two years at 3 per cent interest.

Until they have put their farms on a paying basis, these new immigrant settlers earn a living by building the houses they are going to live in and the farm buildings, surveying the area, digging trenches for water-pipes and laying the pipes, preparing the soil, making roads and so on.

They plough and sow the fields collectively. Every so often a man will take some days off from his paid work to plant vegetables and fodder for his cow. Fruit trees are planted and chickens reared, and as the farm develops, its owner spends more time working on it and less on outside paid jobs.

The country can be divided into four regions:

(a) The central plain, at sea level. There are plentiful water resources not far below the surface, and the land is easy to work. This region extends from Haifa to Be'er Tuvia and includes the coastal strip.

(b) Galilee, including the Jezreel-Jordan Valleys, from Haifa to Safed and Metullah. The soil is heavy, and there is less water here. Wells are much deeper, and water is also piped for greater distances, making it more expensive. The land is harder to work than in the central plain, and yields are smaller. Citrus cannot be grown here. The country is mountainous, so mechanised farming is far less in evidence. Preparation of the soil is hard work and expensive.

(c) The Jerusalem corridor and its environs. The ground here is rocky and hilly. The hills are planted with trees of various kinds, and as the water has to be pumped to quite a height it is expensive. All cultivated land has to be terraced against erosion. The region is cold and rainy and has a heavy dewfall. The main crops here are vegetables and late-ripening fruits.

(*d*) The Negev, from Be'er Tuvia southwards to Eilat. The area between Be'er Tuvia and Beersheba does not have more than twelve inches of rainfall a year. From Beersheba onwards the land is parched desert. The area of settlement has not extended beyond Beersheba. Water has been brought that far, but it is expensive. The soil is good but it has been desert for generations, and so far not many crops have been tried out on it. The land is heavy and the topsoil is limy and very fine.

Since the State of Israel was established there has been mass settlement in all four regions. Natural conditions and the soil determine the economic situation of the farms in the different regions. The central region is the most fruitful. Because of this and also the fact that settlers in this region were given financial assistance and equipment more quickly than elsewhere, new settlement has concentrated there. The biggest proportion of all the produce grown in the country's new settlements comes from the central region.

Development is slower in Galilee and the Jerusalem corridor, both because natural conditions are not so favourable and because those responsible for these regions have not carried out their functions so effectively.

In the Negev, farming development could only begin when water was brought to the area, and it is expensive. Taking into account the difficult conditions and unavoidable delays, progress here has been appreciable too.

In Galilee, the Jerusalem region and the Negev the settlers earn their living from their farms and from outside work. Those who had been able to develop their farms to a greater extent have managed to obtain high prices for the vegetables they have grown and have made very good profits, but there are not many of them.

In the north, most of the young settlements have made very great progress and they are well on the way to economic comsolidation. Most of them are self-supporting to the extent of two-thirds of their needs, while some farmers have made so much progress that they no longer need to take outside jobs. They live from the proceeds of their farms, even before the trees they have planted have begun to bear fruit.

All the problems with which we are beset can be summed up

in one short phrase—bringing the Jews back to the land. Settling 30,000 families on the land is no mean achievement, and the Government and Jewish Agency deserve full credit for it. Villages have been built in many different parts of the country, water pipes laid and farms established and developed. In contrast to many other countries, where there is a movement away from the land to the towns, here in Israel city dwellers are going out to the wastelands to live there and make them bloom. Understanding of the extent and value of this revolutionary phenomenon has not always been forthcoming. We of the second and third waves of immigration have always worked to extend the number of settlements, regardless of our standard of living and the amenities available. Meanwhile general standards have risen considerably. In the past, people who lived in the city had much the same standard of living as the country folk. Today, city dwellers live in luxury and do not work nearly as hard as the rural population. This has resulted in the 15% of immigrants who have gone on the land envying the 85% who have settled in the towns, and there have been cases of new settlers leaving their farms and going to the towns. This trend can only be reversed by bringing conditions in the country up to those in the towns. Living accommodation must be improved, and so must schools, health services and communications. Electrification must be speeded up and there must be more police and guards, so that settlers themselves need not do guard duty; just as city-dwellers have no need to.

When the various branches of agriculture have established themselves on a profitable basis, and Government price subsidies are progressively reduced, farmers will have to become experts. At the moment agricultural work is a closed book to the new immigrant settlers.

Organised marketing alone is not enough either. It must conform to the needs of the new settlers. Their produce must be weighed and paid for on the spot, or even in advance.

Only a third of the farms have been given a cow, and very many fewer than this have been given any poultry. They have begun to plant citrus and other fruit trees and have also been allotted a certain number of abandoned groves, but the new settlers are principally engaged in vegetable growing although here and there a start has been made with groundnuts. The country's cattle population increases by a thousand head a year. The older settlements sell their surplus on the open market, so milch cows are slaughtered instead of being acquired by the settlement authorities for distribution to new settlements.

Most of the new settlers are uneducated. Fifty per cent of the women cannot read or write, nor can many of the men. In the evenings they sit in darkness, unable to read and without anyone to teach them or guide them. The educated members of the old settlements have not gone out among the new settlers, so today we have two nations in Israel—one with fairly high mental and spiritual standards, and one living in utter ignorance. The little that has been done to change this state of affairs by our movement, the Histadrut and the Government is not enough. Clubs and community halls must be built, and the settlers given instruction. Special attention must be paid to the education of the children and young people.

No nation has yet had to face the problem of absorbing people from so many different countries and backgrounds. All the different groups will mingle and flow together, but it will take years. Only when a new generation grows up will the boys and girls who compose it love their people and their country, regardless of their origin.

This problem is nothing new. In this country Sephardim, Ashkenazim, Yemenites, Bokharans and others have lived for many years and have kept their separate identities even into the second and third generations. But new immigrants who established settlements five or six years ago are already beginning to speak Hebrew. Although many of the adults speak their mother tongue among themselves, they speak Hebrew with other immigrants hailing from a different country. Hebrew is the language of general meetings too, because it is the only language a Jew from Germany has in common with one from Turkey, the Yemen or Kurdistan. All their children speak Hebrew too, because it is the language they are taught in and use at school.

What then unites the Jews and keeps them together? The fact that they belong to the Jewish people, their membership of the Hebrew race; their traditions; national pride in Jewish values despite the terrible things which we have suffered; and their pride in our return to our homeland as a people. There is no point in the Jews of America denying their Jewishness, for we are as cultured as any of the American nations and our lineage is as distinguished. The authorities need Jewish votes and Jewish public opinion.

As to whether there is assimilation in America, the answer is clear. The life of most American Jews is no different from that of their non-Jewish neighbours, and it is only logical for assimilation to take place. Nevertheless, despite all logical considerations, young American Jews of the third and fourth generation were inspired by the establishment of the State of Israel and volunteered to fight in the War of Liberation. They contribute appreciable sums to Israel fund-raising activities too, and their feeling for Israel is a strong one. American Jews' financial aid to Israel has exceeded all estimates, and although there may have been special reasons for this, they do not alter the fact.

The State of Israel is working towards the aim of providing a home for half the Hebrew people—at least five million of them. Her economic existence and security alike demand this. The settlement needs of the country and the absence of immigration from elsewhere compel us to direct our energies towards American Jewry. We must initiate a programme of training and preparation for immigration to Israel and settlement there. This will demand tremendous effort and large financial expenditure. Language is the key to mutual understanding. There must be a Hebrew press, Hebrew schools, translations of Hebrew literature, propaganda and publicity on the radio, in the press and through books and pamphlets written in a popular style. Information offices must be established, and selected representatives sent to America for a number of years. There they would choose suitable American Jewish collaborators for their task of bringing about a fundamental revolution in the attitude of American Jewry. If all these things were done in conjunction with one another, the flow of immigration to Israel from America would be increased to a scale compatible with the size of the Jewish community there.

Nahalal is built in the form of a circle. When you reach the circular road, turn right, and you will reach the Dayan house. The two highest trees in the village mark the entrance.

During weekdays, in the cottage behind the small house, active life goes on. Shmuel's daughter, and her husband and three children live there. They are the second and third generations in Nahalal, and maintain the farm.

At weekends the old man comes home. He takes off his suit (he never wears a tie) and changes into grey overalls, the same type worn years ago, the type of overalls that saw the Jordan valley conquered, the marshes dried, the war won, happiness and sorrow. He will go to the cowshed, to the stables, to some work in the orchard, planting, harvest—again and again.

His hair is white now, and his skin is bronzed. His hands are very strong still.

He is alone in the small house. Devora died of cancer a few years ago, his son Moshe entered public service—as a soldier, and now as a politician, and lives away from Nahalal. His daughter lives in a separate house; we, the grandchildren, pay occasional visits. It is a simple house; wooden floor, a large table and few chairs, some beds, a home-made bookcase in which one can notice a few Russian classics and Hebrew books of all sorts—from books on farming to Plato and Descartes. Occasionally I find a children's book from which my grandmother used to read stories to me on long Nahalal winter nights.

Opposite the house is a large grapefruit tree, some grass, a rose garden and a bush of jasmine flowers, all filling the air with wonderful odours. The only decorations on the house walls are family photographs—Shmuel and Devora thirty years ago, twenty, ten years ago....children—Moshe aged three, Aviva in the vegetable garden, Zorik before his death.

There is a small table in the dining room, two candles and a photograph of Zorik, the youngest son. He was killed at the beginning of the War of Independence. He was 21 when he died and left one son, a few months old. To his picture was added Devora's, my grandmother.

But the man is not lonely, and the house is not really empty, for such a full creative life cannot leave a person lonely and a house packed with memories, with sounds and smells of past and future, birth and death and birth again, cannot be empty.

INDEX